Joy in the Journey:

Finding Laughter and Miracles in Very Dark Places

Lisa Jernigan Bain

My precious Mother … Joy through her journey

About Me

Hi friends! Well if you would have told me a few years ago that I would be sitting here writing a book...I would not have believed you. I think I have learned more during this season of my life than ever. 2010 began a journey that would take me on one of the biggest faith walks with the Lord I have ever walked. Faith in God has taken on a whole new meaning. The desert is a hard place to walk but the lessons learned in the dry seasons are life changing. Isaiah 45:3 rang more true in my life than ever. There truly are hidden treasures and secret riches in the dark places. There can be joy in the desert! I hope that some of my words will be an encouragement to someone, and they too can see that whatever journey is waiting for you....you will find joy, you will find grace, and you will find Jesus.

The comedians of the family

Never a dull moment!

Gracie-Anne, Mavis Pearl, Holly Jolly

The Joys of my life!   My Treasures

Follow my Blog! - *http://joyinthejourney-lisa.blogspot.com*

Dedication

I dedicate this book to my precious Mother. Without her, there would be no journey. Her diagnosis of ovarian cancer has taken us down many roads we never thought we would see, yet alone live. Her strength, her faith in the Lord, her ability to laugh in the toughest of situations, her desire to use whatever is in her path as an opportunity to bless others, has changed my life.

I began writing the day I found out she had ovarian cancer. It has helped me look back and see that even in the darkest places, there is joy. Even on the days the tears can't be held back, there is ever sustaining peace in God's presence. We look back on this journey with thankfulness. We cherish life in a way we never have. Our priorities and perspectives have changed. We have realized that sometimes the miracle comes on the journey, not in the destination.

Thank you Mom, for being my hero. There truly is nobody like you. Thank you for this journey. Thank you for walking it out with such grace. I am forever changed because of you.

Table of Contents

Thursday, June 10, 2010

"The Joy of the Lord is My Strength!"

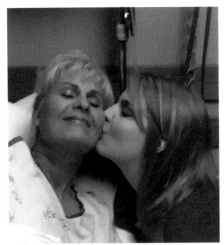

As I sit here in my bed, recovering from major surgery, I am reflective and grateful. Grateful that I just got the great news that all test results, biopsies, and pathologies came out perfect. I love the word benign! It is from heaven to hear those words! This rest time has given me time to write, to put down on paper thoughts that I don't want to forget. Thoughts that have shaped my year.

This year has been filled with many life changing events that have affected my entire family.

One of my favorite phrases is "I may not like what I am going through, but I love what I am becoming because of it."

This year has taught me things that will forever be etched into my spirit. I have learned to never say never. As I sat by myself in the waiting room with the doctor telling me that my mom was filled with cancer... I felt God's grace holding me up. As I had to be the one to tell my father, that his precious wife had cancer... God's grace held me up. As I was told I would need immediate surgery and it was the same surgery my mother had only weeks previously... God's grace held me up. Those of you who know me know how precious my mother and father are to me. In my mind they would live forever. When I got a glimpse in a split second that life was so very fragile, and what I would walk through with my mother would be a difficult journey... my first thought was "Lord, I can't do this!" His response to me was "Lisa, not only do you have the strength to do this, but you will find joy in this journey that has been placed before you." What? Are you kidding me? He wasn't. Not only have I found joy in some very hard places, I have found laughter... much laughter. I see the things that matter in life, and have learned to focus on those things. Life is short. Getting caught up in petty issues takes away the time that really matters... focusing on what is important.

I have also learned to quit asking the Lord, "Why?" Some things I may never know the answer to, but I know His plan is good, and I know that what He sees as the entire picture, may be very different that what I see. His puzzle pieces of my life fit perfectly in place. My use of hammering each piece into place doesn't cut it. His picture is perfect. So I have learned to lay the hammer aside, take a deep breath and trust. Little by little I get a glimpse of the amazing puzzle He is creating in my life. The pieces of my life that were the hardest are some of the most important pieces in my life puzzle.

I have begun to catch a glimpse of the vastness of God's greatness this year in more ways than I can even begin to express. I have been blown away by that glimpse and realize I have only scratched the surface. He is my passion!

So for today as I am on my 3rd day after surgery, recovering... I am finding joy in the very deep place of His presence. This joy doesn't come from people, or things, or circumstances... it comes straight from the heart of Jesus. I pray everyday for those who are hurting to be able to tap into that life sustaining joy and walk boldly and freely through the journey that awaits.

6

We were not promised that we would never face hard times, but we were promised He would be right there with us, holding us, loving us, and filling us with the grace we need to walk through the journey... with joy! The joy of the Lord truly is my strength! Neh. 8:10

I hope you have a joyful week this week, and I pray that you belly laugh! Oh those belly laughs just feel so good!

Laugh away!!!!

Wednesday, June 16, 2010
"Merry Christmas" in June!

I treasure my morning talks with my sweet Mother. My Mother had such a special relationship with her mom. I remember growing up knowing that at around 7:30 every morning they would be on the phone, making sure the other was okay. I never thought much about those daily conversations until my sweet Grandmother went to be with Jesus. I missed those calls, and I know my Mother longed for that phone to ring, and to hear my Grandmother's voice. I thank the Lord that I now have that same relationship with my Mom. Our calls are like clockwork, every morning I hear her voice, and her encouragement for the day just blesses my heart. The journey of her cancer has made those calls even more special to me. Her faith has never wavered, her passion for Jesus has only grown...and she daily inspires me. Today we talked about how much we have learned through this journey together. We have learned more than ever that life is truly a gift. Everyday is a gift to be treasured. When I got off of the phone, in my spirit I saw wrapped presents everywhere! Beautifully wrapped gifts with delicately tied bows of all colors. And I ever so gently heard the Lord say to my heart... "It's Christmas today!"

Do I wake up every morning anxiously ready to open up a new gift hand delivered by my Savior, or do I just sit on the side of the bed looking at all the gifts and go on about my day not receiving what He gave me that day... a gift... a new gift! How many gifts have I missed because I was too focused on things that were so petty. How many times did I say "Why Lord?" when all the time He had the answer right there in front of me... I just didn't open it up and find it! Do many of my gifts have dust on them? Isn't it amazing what we learn in the hardest times of our lives? I have learned so deeply during this incredibly challenging season of my life... that life IS a gift! I don't want to leave one gift unopened... He put them there just for me, to help me, to guide me through each and every day of my journey.

His passion for me is indescribable. It reminds me of how I used to be on Christmas morning when I wanted the kids to hurry and wake up so I could give them their gifts and see the delight on their faces. I couldn't wait to hear the squeals of delight! I think I got more joy than the kids did! That is how Jesus feels about me!

It may be July 16, but in my heart it is December 25th. It's Christmas! A day to open up with excitement, with delight, with passion! This day is to be savored... as if it were my last. Life is so very short... so fragile. So today as I unwrap the gift of today that is before me, I hope you will join me! Let's be like kids on Christmas morning, let's enjoy this day and all that God has waiting for us! I can hear the giggles now, and most of all I can see the indescribable joy on my savior's face as we receive from Him all He has for us. What a wonderful Savior I serve!

Merry Christmas!

"Yesterday is history, tomorrow is a mystery, today is God's gift, that's why we call it the present."

Wednesday, June 23, 2010

When Your Tears Are Your Prayer

 I was thinking about a precious lady I met years ago on one of my singing tours who had just been diagnosed with stage 4 cancer. Her heart was broken, she was paralyzed with fear. I remember during ministry time she came up to me and fell into my arms sobbing. She then whispered in my ear... "I don't know how to pray those big worded prayers that God hears, so what do I do?" I remember holding her face in my hands and telling her those tears were her prayer, her heart's cry was a prayer that went straight to the heart of Jesus. I am always taken back to that time when no words come... only the cry of my heart. God has never failed to hear that cry and come running to my rescue. Some of the greatest miracles in my life came when all I could say was "Jesus help!", or when tears took over and words couldn't come. Those tears were all I had... God knew. Oh and did I mention that the precious lady I got to know that evening is serving God today... cancer free! He hears the cry of your heart, and He will coming running... He will answer... a miracle awaits!

Saturday, July 31, 2010

"Shall We Dance?"

It's been 8 weeks! Eight weeks since my surgery and I got the Dr.'s "OK" to run again! My running shoes were beckoning me to get out there again and get back to my normal daily runs. As I tied up the shoe laces anticipating that great adrenaline rush I had not felt for 8 weeks, I realized I had a new outlook on it all. A new excitement to just enjoy!

As I began the run... I got so excited to be out there again, I just began to do a victory dance as I ran. My arms up in the air, a skip to my step, and a few turns with some groove moves here and there kept me going... :) I heard a voice in the distance say "MOMMY, what's wrong with that lady?" I knew this little girl's mother, and heard her mother come out to see, and replied with a chuckle to her daughter "Carly, that's just Lisa... she does happy dances!" I slowed down to listen to this conversation and heard Carly ask if she could do one too! By this time I was by her mother and said I'd love Carly to join me! So we danced... and we danced... and we DANCED! And passers by were quite amused; one little old man walking by even waved his cane around with a groove like none I'd seen. By the time it was all done we had a group of neighbors, laughing and dancing their own jig with us! Some quite hilarious, but that made it all the more wonderful!

On my run home from my wonderful dance with Carly, I felt the smile of Jesus just radiating... He was dancing too! You see, as I look back on that dance in my neighborhood, he brought to my attention... "Lisa, think on all those dancing with you..." I stopped in my tracks. I knew all of the neighbors dancing. One lady was a precious caretaker of her terminally ill husband; one just said goodbye to her son going to Iraq; one had a prosthesis from an injury from the war, and was dancing away as best he could; one lady just lost her mother; one man had just had a heart attack 2 months earlier and was struggling with depression. I knew every single one of these people... and their stories all filled with such HUGE hurdles... They made my hurdles look so small.

When I got home I had a message on my phone from the lady taking care of her husband. I speak with her frequently. She thanked me for the dance. She said she got a glimmer of how we need to dance in the dark times, and thank God for the little things in life. It may just be a little dance... but it's a dance. It's a light that can spread in a dark situation. She was crying at this point... and so was I. We had a chance to pray together on the phone. I just love her so much! Once again, God teaches me.

Look at what one dance can do! Do I look for those dances in the dark times? It's been a summer of many hurdles for our family. From my Mother's cancer, to my health scare and surgery, to saying some hard goodbyes, and seeing my sister move to Canada. These were hurdles, but the lessons I have learned I would not trade for the world. I have learned to dance! And I am learning how to dance over hurdles. I may not win a track competition for hurdles, but I know I would have more fun than anyone else in the competition! Isn't that what God would love us all to grasp onto anyway? It's not about the journey... it's about how we go through that journey that makes us stronger! Jesus gives us the "dance"! He gives us the grace to hurdle in spite of how high that hurdle is. Loneliness, Pain, Rejection, Disease, Grief, Anger, Broken Marriages, A Lost Loved One, Addiction, Low Self-Esteem... whatever that hurdle is, God not only has a way over that hurdle, but one that will even surprise you!

I am learning that the biggest hurdle in my life is really not so big when Jesus is right there on the other side ready to catch me. If I don't eloquently dance, or leap over it... if I fall flat on my face... He catches me and finishes the race with me... dancing! I finish victoriously!

There are days I have no dance in my step... days I would love to give up and have a pity party... but I have found that all it takes is putting one step in front of the other, crying out to Jesus for His help, and He takes it from there. Before I know it that one foot in front of the other... has turned to into a dance.

The breakthrough has begun.

If it's a dance from the heart, a dance from the soul, or a physical dance... it's a dance.

It's a place of letting go and letting God. It's such a precious place to be.

Shall we dance?

Sunday, September 12, 2010

Heavenly Novocaine

Whoever questions whether there is a God or not and how amazing his power is, should have been on my run with me this morning with Holly. We started our run and about 10 minutes into it Holly got in front of me and braced (what service dogs do when a partner is needing support to get up) I almost fell over her. She never does this on our runs. I was frustrated at her after about the 5th time she did it. Why was she doing this? It was out of her character! It then occurred to me that she may be trying to get me to turn around for some reason. Was she warning me? So I turned around and sure enough down the street came a HUGE German shepherd and a pit bull. They were coming straight for us. As they got closer I saw foam out of both of their mouths and teeth showing. Uh, not a good sign. You know, it is in moments like these that you wet your pants and then your life flashes before your eyes. I felt an adrenaline rush like never before and I pushed Holly behind me and I was going to take them on!

Uh, yeah right.

I looked quickly around all sides for their owners... I thought about running, no time....we were stuck. Holly got back in front of me as soon as I pushed her behind. She was trying to protect me with everything in her.

I finally was the one in front when the German shepherd went around to her head and got her neck in his teeth. The pit bull got her from behind. I started kicking and pulling... and knew this was not going to end well. One of us was going to be chewed up! They had a grip of death on Holly and they were not going to let go. Then all of the sudden I just yelled as loud as I could... "IN THE NAME OF JESUS, LET GO NOW!!! JESUS HELP ME PLEASE!" And believe me, the neighborhood heard that scream. I think all of heaven and earth heard that scream. All of the sudden the dogs dropped. OK, now when I say they dropped, it was like they were shot with Novocaine. Like nothing I'd ever seen. By this time my legs were shaking so hard Holly really WAS holding me up. She was calm, she was now in front of me braced. I was saying under my breath... about a million "thank you Jesus's..." We stepped over the dogs... and we ran like we never ran before. I got to the curb and checked Holly out... she was not bleeding, her hips were ok. That alone was a miracle! A neighbor ran down to meet me and said it was a miracle we made it out of that one alive. She asked me how I got the dogs down. I said "Did you hear my scream to Jesus? Well it worked!" Her mouth was hanging open.

I looked down the street and the dogs had been retrieved by 2 people. They were on leashes now and kind of wobbly. I didn't know whether to laugh or cry. Oh, if I could have seen from heaven's point of view all that was happening at that very moment... it would have blown my mind! God's hand, His angels, His arms... protecting all the way... stopping those dogs in their tracks and laying them down. Thank God for heavenly Novocaine! I have thought about this event all morning long. I have thought about how immediately at the mention of the name of Jesus... He was there. I have replayed it over and over and over in my head.

Holly is laying under my feet as I type this. She was my brave angel today... she tried to warn me many times to turn around, but I didn't. Next time... I'll heed the warnings.

God's faithfulness blows me away. His protection, His provision, His miracles to be there through it all... are mind boggling. I had a conversation with a person the other day who was a friend of a friend. He was challenging me of God's existence. We talked for hours! I truly believe if that young man had been with me today, there would be no question in his mind.

Friday, October 8, 2010

As I sat on the doctor's table realizing my shoes didn't match... I just laughed. A year ago, that would have sent me running home to get the right ones on my feet. But now? Nahhh I think I'll go with it all day. I have learned to not sweat the small stuff this year. Mismatching shoes would definitely fall into that category. As the doctor came in to check me out, I saw the grimace on his face when he looked at me. I was like "Ok, God... it's small stuff right?" He said I was not healing correctly and he would give it a few more weeks to keep doing what he was doing to fix it, but if it was not doing better... more surgery. But wait! I have another surgery in November before Thanksgiving! That would mean 4 surgeries in 3 months. I want to be in the fruit of the month club, not surgery of the month club! I sat there looking at him and I just laughed. Didn't know what else to do! I heard the Lord whisper in my ear... "regroup or regret Lisa... you have a choice." HUH? That didn't make sense to me. But now it does. I am a planner! And I love the holidays so much it is not even funny. I start decorating for Christmas November 1st! This was not in my plans! In fact this messed up my plans! It was then I realized....I don't want to regret the things I do in life and the choices I make. I want to savor the seconds because it can all change so fast. I don't want regrets. I needed to regroup.

I looked at my calendar, laid hands on it and prayed. "Lord... if the things on this calendar go as planned... Hooray! If they do not, you plan them out in a way that will be glorious! The plans may change, but it will all be good. I will trust you." If surgery is on your calendar for me to get well... so be it. If you choose to heal me miraculously... Hooray again! I trust you. COMPLETELY trust you. This year of Mom's cancer journey and my surgery journey... no words can adequately describe. Growth in ways I never expected. Relationship with Jesus like I never knew before. Amazing things can happen in truly dark places. His light makes those dark places so brilliant. There are things seen there that we would never see otherwise.

So as I walked out of the doctor's office with my mismatched shoes on... I smiled to myself, knowing God has it all in His hands. I felt His sweet presence. I have learned that peace is not the absence of affliction, but the presence of God. I felt peace.

I am planning on decorating for Christmas November 1st, and I am planning fun parties with the kids. If God has other plans... I know they will be amazing! He has never let me down. His calendar is filled with glorious things for me! If it took this journey to get me to this place with Him... it was worth it.

Now, up to the attic to start unloading the Christmas wreaths! YES!

Friday, November 5, 2010

Jesus Loves Me... This I Know

Once again I am sitting in my bed with my laptop recovering from hopefully my last surgery! I have my dogs snuggled up with me and a husband that is the best nurse ever! I am thankful.

This journey has been quite a journey. And you know I can look back through this year and see God's hand prints all over the place. We are never promised a tomorrow, and I have realized more than ever to savor every second of today. God's peace is there in the dark places. Many of my friends have faced tragedies this year, and I have seen God meet them in such a precious way. It truly is the peace that passes all understanding. What would we do without that precious peace! Peace is not the absence of affliction, but the presence of God.

We are entering the holiday season... my favorite time of year. I am one of those people who decorate very early. Nothing like eating Thanksgiving dinner by the Christmas Tree! Since I had this surgery so early, I decorated even earlier than usual. I had the most precious friend help me. Emma Hardin, you made decorating day a day I will never forget! I finally found someone who loves the holidays as much as I do! Fun, joy, baking, decorating, and silly dances filled the day! I am so thankful.

I have had a lot of time to reflect, and pray during all this recovery time. It's been so good for me. I have fallen in love with Jesus in a whole new way. I will not think of 2010 as a year of hard journeys, but as a year where I saw Jesus in ways I never dreamed. It was a year of seeing huge miracles. But mostly it was a year where I felt His presence in the midst of the storm.

They said when I came out of anesthesia this time from surgery I had my arms up in the air and was singing "Jesus Loves Me". Yep, peace is not the absence of affliction but the presence of God. How many times have I sung Jesus Loves Me throughout my life? Many. But this year the reality of how very much He truly loves me... soaked in.

He loves me enough to carry me when I can't walk, see for me when my sight is blurred, dance over me with singing, when I can't dance. He lifts me up when I can't jump the hurdles, carries me when I am under anesthesia and holds me close, and blesses me with such beautiful friendships to pray with me and be an extension of His arms when I need them. I have learned that some days when there is not a song in my heart... sing anyway. Jesus always gives me a new song to sing.

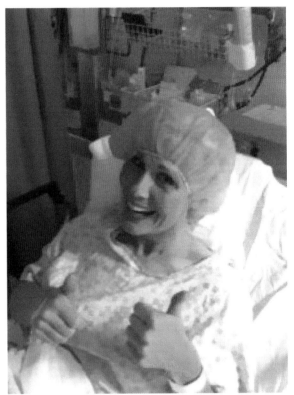

Jesus loves me! this I know,
For the Bible tells me so.
Little ones to Him belong;
they are weak but He is strong.

Yes, Jesus loves me!
Yes, Jesus loves me!
Yes, Jesus loves me!
The Bible tells me so.

Sing that song today.....sometimes it's the simple little things, that make profound differences in our heart. Jesus loves you.....really really loves you!

Tuesday, November 9, 2010

Heaven Came to Visit Today…

The holiday season always brings me such joy. I am always taken back to the days when I was a little girl and my grandma would be baking away in the kitchen. She always had a pot of boiled custard, peanut brittle, and divinity in the making. I remember she always had straight pins in her collar where she could easily get to them as she sewed missions clothes for the little children who had none. But today the memory that stood out in my mind was a song she would hum. She hummed many songs under her breath everyday. She loved the Gaither's. I used to call those songs she sang "old people songs". But today... it was one of those "old people songs" that brought heaven very close. I think heaven is closer than we realize. Days like today, I am convinced of it. The pain from this surgery has been more than I expected. It's been a time of complete surrender to the Lord to know... He's got it... He will take it for me... and I can rest. Feeling a little discouraged with the recovery process, I plugged in my iPod this morning before I started reading and a song came on... did I put it on there? I didn't remember doing so. But immediately the harmony resounded... Oh that beautiful harmony that is rarely heard these days in songs anymore... it was my Grandma's favorite song.

Shackled by a heavy burden,
'Neath a load of guilt and shame.
Then the hand of Jesus touched me,
And now I am no longer the same.

He touched me, Oh He touched me,
And oh the joy that floods my soul!
Something happened and now I know,
He touched me and made me whole.

Since I met this blessed Savior,
Since He cleansed and made me whole,
I will never cease to praise Him,
I'll shout it while eternity rolls.

He touched me, Oh He touched me,
And oh the joy that floods my soul!
Something happened and now I know
He touched me and made me whole.

I smiled as I sang this song over and over and over... I know Grandma was singing with me. And I know she was smiling at me as I sang at the top of my lungs this "old people song" I used to tease her about.

This year has opened my eyes to so many things in the heavenly realm. When faced with the fragility of life, and how quickly things can change... it's that complete surrender to Jesus that brings us so close to His heart that you can feel His breath on your face. I have had many friends walk through tragedy this year... I have seen hearts break. But at the other side of it all, I have seen heaven come down in ways I never dreamed possible.

I closed my eyes after the song was over... took a deep breath, and then realized... I could take a deep breath. Before the song... it was too painful. I breathed the deepest breath I could breathe and filled my lungs with air that didn't hurt! I wiped the tears away... knowing that in this few minutes singing... heaven really visited me today... in my room, with my Grandma... and angels were singing with her. His healing touch... His healing presence... left me speechless.

He touched me, Oh He touched me,
And oh the joy that floods my soul!
Something happened and now I know
He touched me and made me whole.

Sunday, November 14, 2010

Home Sweet Home

I just read my sister's blog... she amazes me. Her blog was about "home". I was sitting there reading it shouting "Yes!" I think this time of year really hits "home" for a lot of people. What is home? I have to quote my sister on this one because I feel exactly the same way she does:

"Home is an important place--especially when it's cold outside. It's somewhere that I know I'll be warm and safe, but it's more than that. It's where my family is. It's a place where I can hang around in my pajamas, forget about putting on makeup and no one will vote me off the island. I have a lifetime membership with this clan--warts and all."

I remember as a little girl going to camp. I was so homesick I thought I would die! I remember the embarrassment of having the camp counselor call my parents to come and pick me up. It was humiliating but I will never forget laying in the back seat after they picked me up, and feeling complete peace... knowing I was going home. It was worth the embarrassment. To this day I use the expression "I am having one of those I want to go home from camp moments".

As precious as my home is to me, I am realizing more and more that home is truly where my heart is. Our family has faced a multitude of transitions and hurdles this year. Seeing my son move to Nashville and my sister move to Canada were big hurdles for me. Mom's cancer, Skipper's retirement, and my health issues this year caused our family to go through even more transition. At one point I felt like this was the worst season of my life. I felt like I had been punched in the gut and couldn't breathe! I was having a "camp" moment. I felt lost!

Then the Lord so sweetly showed me that it wasn't these times that defined my home... it was His presence in my heart that was my defining "safe place".

This time of year can bring "home" to a whole new light. Family and home can represent complete joy and safety for some, while for others it represents pain, abandonment, hopelessness and loneliness. I have a burden on my heart to pray for those who are hurting during this time of year. I know God wants to be that safe place and redefine "home" for them.

One of my favorite songs is by Bryan Duncan, "When I Think of Home". Here is one of the verses:

"There's a saying: your home is where your heart is....My heart believes its true,
and my home's so far away. But the seasons and the scenery keep changing, So I'll make my home with you, 'Til I'm finally home to stay.
When I think of home, When I'm tired and feeling homeless, I come to you....
You're where my heart is."

I will end on this quote from my sister......it says it all:

"Family is powerful. It's the vessel that God chose to usher Jesus into the world when it was very cold and dark outside. Even though Jesus is now preparing a forever-home for me in heaven, His Spirit lives inside of me here on earth and I'm never separated from His presence. No matter what changes, no matter where I go, the presence of God is always with me. That's my real home--that's my happy place."

I want to post my sister's blog address: Her blogs are amazing...
I often steal quotes from her. Thank you Julie! I want to be like you when I grow up!

http://prayervitamins.blogspot.com/

Wednesday, December 1, 2010

Live Out Loud

I saw my precious elderly neighbor walk slowly with her cane, to the curbside to get her paper this morning. It was then that my mind filled with special memories of yet another neighbor. We call him Mr. Bob. Mr. Bob lost his wife years ago and lived by himself. I have learned more things from the life of Mr. Bob... Life changing things... he lived out loud.

Every morning without fail, very very early, you would find Mr. Bob walking to each house, picking up the newspaper, and taking it to their front door. I have watched Mr. Bob do this for many years. I watched him as he walked briskly to each door, then after hip and knee replacements, he walked with a cane to each door. The final weeks of his life, Mr. Bob had his walker, and he was determined to get each paper to each door. Some days it would take him hours... he just started earlier. I have seen him walk through rain, snow, sleet and hail literally... to get that newspaper to the door. I always loved my conversations with Mr. Bob. He always, and I do mean always, had a smile on his face and exuded joy.

I offered to help him on days I knew he was going very slowly and knew he was hurting. (Although he would never admit it) He would always tell me he was fine and loved doing this, it brought him joy. I asked about his determination to do this everyday. He said to me "Lisa, it may be a very small thing, but over the years I have learned that it is not by what you say that reaches most people, but how you live. I want to live out loud... I want to love out loud... without saying a word." He then went on to tell me that he prayed for each house and their family as he put each paper by the door. He said to me that over the years he has reached more people for Jesus without saying a word... just living what he believed. The thing I remember so vividly about Mr. Bob was the light that you could see and feel in his life. His eyes beamed. He always had a wave for every passing car. Many times I could hear him singing and whistling as he was delivering papers. It was hard to see Mr. Bob pass away recently. He was 87 years young when he died. Oh I so loved that man. He was like a grandfather to the neighborhood. It was a sad day, the day Mr. Bob went to be with Jesus.

As I took Holly for a walk this morning, I saw all the papers out with frost on them. A sight that I was not used to seeing. Oh how we miss Mr. Bob. It was then that I saw my sweet elderly neighbor walk ever so slowly to the curb to get her paper. Holly was carrying her leash in her mouth and promptly ran over to my neighbor, dropped her leash, and picked up the paper. At first I was chasing after her thinking Holly was going to scare my precious friend. It was then that I just heard the Lord say to my heart... let her go... listen Lisa, watch... love... it's your turn. I was like HUH? So I stopped, watched Holly go get the paper in her mouth, and she walked that paper up to the front door and she waited for my neighbor to get to the door. My neighbor was delighted! She was so happy and said this made her day. She was laughing and waving her arms with excitement. Holly handed her the paper with her mouth, and wagged that tail with more joy than I have ever seen. Holly knew....she knew! Me? I was standing in the street, mouth open, tears streaming down my face, watching my dog literally be used by God! Sounds funny huh? It was my turn. It was my turn to live out loud. I got it. And God used my dog to help me "get it."

We would take over where Mr. Bob left off. We just finished getting the papers on our street, took them up to each door, via Holly and her happy tail. She had the time of her life. And you know what? So did I. Mr. Bob was right... this was fun. It gives me time to pray for each house, each neighbor, and have more time to just listen. Mr. Bob is up there in heaven I know, smiling. I kind of think he prayed for this before he went to be with Jesus. He lived out loud... I want that too! I am happy Holly and I can follow in his footsteps... literally.

Friday, December 24, 2010

It's Christmas Eve. My dogs are snuggled at my feet, and the Christmas lights are twinkling, as I am up early with my morning cup of coffee. As I sit here looking at the gifts under the tree, I am taken back to the events of the year. I think about the precious friends I made, the relationships that were established, the victories I walked through with my friends and family, the tears we cried together, the prayers we prayed, and memories we made.

I had a sweet conversation with one of my dear friends last night, and as we talked I was just so thankful I had her. She has always been there to pray with me. She has always been so faithful to be there through every season. I have been so blessed with such wonderful friendships this year.

It was a year filled with hurdles, but I have to say, it was a year with more blessings because of those hurdles. I met people I would never have met. I grew stronger than I thought was even possible. I thought I would come to the end of this year saying to myself... "Wow, that was just a very tough year, and I'm ready for it to be over." That's not what I am saying. This year was a gift. It was a gift that showed me that the real gifts are not those under the tree. It is life, it is my precious friends who I am so thankful for, it is my Mom and Dad who are with me here to celebrate, it's about my loving husband, and my children who I adore... it's about family. Most importantly... it is about Jesus... the lover of my soul... my precious Jesus.

He loved me so much that he came into this world in such a humble way. In a stable, born in a manger (with a lot of poop and bad smells around!) I think about how hard it must have been. But He did if for me. Quite frankly, that blows me away.

My friend and I were talking about our favorite Christmas carols last night. We came to the conclusion that "Oh Holy Night" was our favorite. It sums it all up. What a Holy night it was. A night divine! A night that changed the world... a night that is why I am even here... sitting by this tree... in the quiet of His presence.

So as I sit here quietly in my spirit... I am thankful for the many treasures God gave me this year. They don't require wrapping paper, they don't have any assembly required, and they don't need batteries. These gifts will be here for years to come... they won't be given to Goodwill or thrown away, and they won't break. They are eternal. I have never treasured these gifts more than I do this year. My family... my friends... my Jesus.

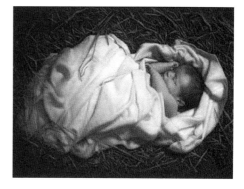

May you all bask in the wonderful gift of Jesus this Christmas and treasure those eternal gifts He gives through friends and family. The treasures that last an eternity.

Merry Christmas!

Tuesday, December 28, 2010

Wild Abandon … Here I Come!

I was off and running in the crisp cold air this morning... with one thing on my mind... thoughts about the New Year. There is so much emphasis on New Year's resolutions... and we know how those go. As I ran this morning I kept thinking about what my year held, and what the next year holds. For some reason my mind kept going back to a story I read in my devotions this morning.

It was about a 17 year old girl who worshiped the Lord with wild abandon! Every Sunday she would be raising her hands, dancing with delight with the light of Jesus shining out of her eyes. She was wholeheartedly worshiping the Lord. The more mature, sedate believers were worshiping God as well...in a refined, upscale kind of way. The young girl's mother would grab her and pull her back to her seat but the young girl didn't care. She wanted to praise God. So her hands stayed in the air and she clapped and sang loudly as she worshiped Him with abandon. The young girl turned out to be a 2 year old trapped in the body of a 17 year old. She was autistic. She hadn't learned that her style of worship should please and impress people. Her worship hadn't been tainted with religious pomp and circumstance. She didn't pay attention to the people around her or worry about what they might think of her. Out of her childlike relationship with her Savior, this young girl just gave Jesus everything she had.

Do I have this childlike relationship with the Lord? Have I become too grown up to receive what Jesus has for me? Too dignified to respond as spontaneously and wholeheartedly to Him as a child would? I don't want anything blocking me from hearing His voice more clearly. I want to worship with wild abandon. After all that is what Jesus does over me! He dances over me with singing! Praise and Worship is near and dear to my heart. It was traveling in groups across the country, and singing praise and worship through music ministry, where I received so much healing in my life. It gets me right to the heart of my Savior. This year I want to worship and serve the Lord with wild abandon. I want to love Jesus with a child like love that goes straight to His heart. I don't want to be a sedate believer.

I have seen a glimpse of Jesus in ways that have been astounding this year through some trials and hurdles that came our way, and I want to tap in deeper. His Holy Spirit is what carried me through when I humanly could not. It was miraculous to say the least.

Whatever 2011 holds, I want to always be reminded of that young girl... praising her Savior with wild abandon. She had a glimpse of heaven. Who can get that glimpse and not stand still?

As I finished my run... I began to run with my arms raised up and a dance to my step. I am excited! I look forward to 2011 whatever it holds. I face it with wild abandon, and know that in His presence... whatever comes my way... He will be smiling over me, and will carry me through to victory. It will be a glorious year in His presence.

2011 Here I come!

Thursday, January 6, 2011

A Day of Beauty!

As I sat there watching my Mother get her hair washed... tears were streaming down my face. Not only did she have hair to wash now... she was radiant! I remember the day like it was yesterday. It was Easter and my Mother called me to tell me that her hair had fallen out in clumps. The chemotherapy's effects had begun. I also remember the day that my Dad shaved my Mother's head.... and I remember him telling her how utterly beautiful she was. We didn't know the future... we didn't know if her hair would ever grow back. But my sweet Mother, never uttered a negative word. Only thankfulness that God knew what He was doing. It was only hair after all. But deep inside I knew it had to be so difficult for my sweet Mom.

For Christmas this year we purchased a gift certificate for my Mom. She would get a full day of beauty from an amazing salon in town. From a facial, to make-up, to a hair cut (she now had hair to cut!)... you name it.... she got it. Today was the day we went together for her Day of Beauty. Little did I know it would turn out to be a day forever etched into my memory... and my heart.

I was quite surprised at how this day affected me. Tears were there at every turn. Some held back, some just came out in spite of my every effort hold them back. When she walked out after her wonderful day of pampering... she was glowing. She was radiant! She was beautiful! I will never forget that picture in my mind...ever. The events of the year and her journey through cancer all raced through my mind on fast forward, and there I was... witnessing my miracle Mom in the present. Just beautiful... with beautiful hair!

We then went to lunch and had such a wonderful time together. The one thing my mom has said to me my entire life, and reiterated today was this: No matter how bad the day gets, no matter how dark it looks in life... there will always be something good to grasp onto. It may be very very small, but there will be something. It may even be as small as a smile that touched your heart. Grab that something with everything you have and focus on that good thing. God will take it from there. A miracle can blossom from that very tiny good thing you found. She lives it everyday, and I have seen it work! I am so thankful she has lived it out for me... it's a heritage I am so thankful for. I am more thankful for it today than ever.

Mom, being the most unselfish lady I know, kept saying to me... "Oh Lisa, I wish you would not have given me such an elaborate gift! You shouldn't have!" And what Mom didn't realize was that what she gave me was the best gift I could have ever received. Watching her joy today, and her beauty just beaming, and being with her... was my gift. The best Christmas gift I have ever received. I will never forget this day. It is my treasure... and so is my Mom.

Monday, February 7, 2011

A "Remote" Journey with Deloris!

 Her name was Deloris, she was 4 1/2 feet tall.... and I had no idea how she would impact my life. As I waited in the emergency room for a bed to open up in the hospital... I was not a happy camper. I did not want to go through yet another hospital adventure. 2011 was not supposed to begin this way! I was hooked up to so many wires that I felt like I was turning into the bionic woman. As I sat there alone in the E.R. I thought to myself... "OK, Lisa, find the humor in this, find the joy in this journey!" Hmmm, as hard as I tried....for some reason having a pity party sounded much better than laughing. All I could do was whimper out a frustrated whisper... "Jesus, help!" But somehow I knew that pathetic whimper of a prayer went straight to the heart of Jesus. Did I feel instant joy and laughter after my prayer? No. But deep inside... I knew He was there...in the midst of my pity party... Jesus was there.

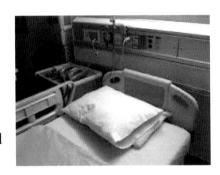

They wheeled me up to the second floor. As they got me settled into bed I heard from behind the curtain... a raspy voice yell "I have the remote to this T.V. and I am the boss of it!" Hmm... I guess that was my welcome to this temporary humble abode I would be in for a few days. Yes, her name was Deloris. She was my roommate. I could only ask the Lord "Why?"... no answer. At that point I only knew 2 things: #1 God had to know what He was doing. #2 Deloris was boss of the T.V. remote (She wasn't kidding either.)

Through the next several days I would go through many medical tests, and so would she. I got to know Deloris. Though that blue medical curtain separated us for the first few hours of our being introduced... it didn't stay up long. We became friends. I realized Deloris was the way she was, stubborn and headstrong, for a reason. Her life story brought me to tears in only a few minutes of her telling that story. It was filled with abandonment, abuse, loneliness, and sadness. She told me later that nobody had ever wanted to hear her story before... this was a first for her. Deloris was a severe diabetic. She had come close to death several times. I sat with her when the nurse from diabetic eduction came up to teach her about changes in her diet, and the severe consequences she would face if she didn't make these changes. I learned a lot from sitting with Deloris that day.

It was my turn for tests, and as I left the room to head downstairs for a stress test... she thanked me for sitting with her and I saw her wipe a tear quickly from her face, not wanting me to see. She will never know what that tear did for my heart.

When I returned from my tests, Deloris was asleep. I got settled into bed and as soon as I lifted up my pillow... there it was! THE T.V. REMOTE! She had given me the remote! I knew how much that remote meant to Deloris, and I knew this was huge for her. I have never been choked up over a remote before in my life, but today... I was. And you know what is funny... I didn't even want to watch T.V. anymore. I quietly reached over and put it back under her pillow. I saw her smile. (Again, she didn't want me to see that smile, but I did.)

On this visit to the hospital I met many people... and as I was wheeled down for tests, the hallway was lined with people waiting to be wheeled into their tests. I saw a lady crying... she was scared... I wanted to hop off of my wheelchair and hug her. It broke my heart to see her crying alone in the corner. It was then that I heard it... that still small voice that carries me through every single day of my life. That quiet voice of the Lord whispered to me... "Lisa, this is why you are here. You will be ok... just pray." These people were not put into my life by chance... they were laid deeply and heavily on my heart to pray for. Could it be that certain things are allowed by the Lord so we are brought into situations that will not only change our lives but the lives of others? The longer I live, the more I find this to be true.

When Deloris was released, I prayed for her... she looked at me this time wiping tears from her face and said... "Lisa, if you ever come to my house to visit, you can always have the remote to my T.V... thank you for listening to my story and for being my friend." I was proud of myself for keeping it all together... until she left. Then I went through a box of Kleenex. I don't think I will ever look at our T.V. remote the same again.

With all the snow we just had in Tulsa, it was a time to be home-bound. One day I was a little melancholy and feeling a little low. I was prompted by the Lord to pray for Deloris, for the others I met at the hospital that day. As I began to pray my spirits lifted... if a heart could smile, mine was smiling. One prayer led to another and before I knew it....those prayers brought a joy to my spirit. There is just something about prayer and praising... you can't stay low for long! That's why the enemy tries so desperately to keep us focused on everything else! Deloris once again made my heart smile. God knew the day I was having my pity party in that E.R. Room... that today... I would be praying for Deloris... and all the others I met that day... and I would be blessed.

Life is filled with journeys. And the longer I live, going through difficult journeys... I am realizing more and more that sometimes God's answer and gift to us is the journey itself.... not the final destination. That journey is what makes us appreciate and cherish the destination when we get there. It's what gives us the maturity to see it the way God sees it. What I have learned this year has changed my life. The people I have met, have impacted me in ways I cannot describe. The Holy Spirit has shown me things, and taught me lessons... even in my pain. Each day is precious.

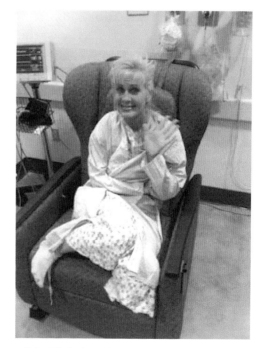

So as I stood in line for 4 hours for groceries before the blizzard of Tulsa hit, listening to angry people mad at the long lines. I felt such a peace as I stood there. When it's all put into perspective... it's a blessing to be able to be standing...to not be in a hospital bed... to be able to buy groceries... to just have another day of life! I am thankful for so many things. I am thankful for friends, for family, for another day to serve Jesus, and of course... for my remote control! I think it's time to go visit my friend... Deloris!

Monday, February 14, 2011

Valentine's Day ….

Valentine's Day... a day of love, hearts, candy, flowers, and fancy dinners. My heart always goes out to those who dread this holiday rather than look forward to it with excitement. In fact I used to be one of those people. I would see January, and know February 14 was on its way. It was like if I didn't have a special valentine, I would be exempt from having fun on this holiday. As a single Mom for many years, just focused on raising my children, Valentine's Day was not on the forefront of my mind. I always go back to those memories on days like today, but I see them differently now. I see how God used the worst of trials to show me His heart, His love for me and how He would use those hard times to make me better, and give me the ability to receive all He had ahead.

I remember sitting at the table with my then 8 year old daughter and 6 year old son, years ago gluing decorations on their Valentine's Day bags for their school party. I was busy trying to figure out if I would be able to take time off from my job to be a homeroom mom for the party I so desperately wanted to attend. My heart was just so torn, and really quite discouraged. I was tired, I was lonely. But I so vividly remember that day like it was yesterday. As I dropped my kids off at school for the day, my little boy handed me something. I was in a hurry and sat it on the car seat knowing I would look at it later.

On the drive to work, I remember praying the day would go quickly. I knew the ladies at work would have a desk full of flowers and candy and cards, and I would get to see them all day, reminding me that I didn't have a Valentine this year.

I started to get out of the car and looked down on my seat and there it was... the card from my son. I sat there behind the building and opened it up. He had hand made me a valentine. It was a heart that he had cut out himself. It said "Mommy, you have the best Valentine's ever... Me, Laura, and Jesus. We love you, Mommy." With words misspelled, and the edges frayed because his scissors were too big, it made it even more special. In fact something grabbed my heart that morning. Something changed my life forever. It was the realization that I was loved, so very loved. I had 2 beautiful children and a God who delighted over me and on this day He was dancing over the very thought of me. He was the lover of my soul... now how does it get any better than that? I had always known God was there, always knew these things to be true... but today, reading this precious little card from my son... it hit home. I mean really hit home.

It was like a life-changing moment when Jesus just grabbed my heart... and I really knew it was His. I may not have had dozens of roses on my desk that day, but that precious card that my son gave me meant more to me than all the flowers in the world. And it stayed on my desk long after Valentine's day. It reminded me who really had my heart.

Years have passed since that Valentine's Day. In fact when I think of how God blessed my life in ways I could never comprehend, I am once again reminded of His great love for me. It's a love that is quite indescribable. God truly gives us the desires of our hearts. The dreams I held onto for those many years... He fulfilled. All that the enemy tried to take from me, God restored. For those of you who know my story, know this to be true. You watched it unfold.

I guess I am writing this blog today because I want to encourage those who do not think they will ever have their breakthrough... that think they will never have a Valentine... and who experience pain on this day instead of happiness. Let Jesus take your heart, and rest in knowing you are loved beyond measure. If your heart is broken... give Him the pieces. He will make it whole again. I know... because He did it for me.

My sweet husband left for work today, but before he left he did as he always does... he wrapped his arms around me and he prayed. He prayed for me, and he thanked God for me, he prayed for our 4 children, and even our 2 dogs. He covered it all. As he left today I was taken back to that day when Jesus grabbed onto my heart so intimately. Look how much He blessed me! Look how far I had come! Oh the joy and blessing of complete surrender to His love. There is no greater love than His.

Don't give up. This is your Valentine's Day today... what He has waiting for you is far greater than flowers or candy. It's your breakthrough... it's your dream. Nobody can take care of your heart better than He can! Happy Valentine's Day!

Wednesday, February 23, 2011

A Walk With Jesus

I remember as a child hearing the verse *"Come to Me all who labor and are heavy laden and I will give you rest... For My yoke is easy to bear, and the burden I give you is light."* I used to think it had to do with eggs... it was quite a perplexing verse to me. Little did I know that the verse in Matthew would be one I would stand on throughout my life.

At one of my doctor visits the other day, during my long wait, I struck up a conversation with a sweet little elderly lady. She was there with her husband, and her spirit drew me to her. I knew she loved the Lord, I just knew... it was written all over her face. And I was correct. Her husband was very ill, yet her trust in God for all she carried blessed my heart. There was peace all around her. She quoted this verse during our conversation, and my heart just smiled. She knew what trust was all about. If ever there was a definition of pure peace in the midst of a horrible storm... her face was the definition. Her spirit exuded complete trust.

There is a word that I heard someone use one day, "efforting." It means struggling unnecessarily in an effort to do something. It could be illustrated by pushing a car to your destination when it would be much easier to start the engine and drive it. I wish I could say that I never did this... but indeed I have. This year I have learned that complete trust is far greater than my "efforting." Jesus was waiting there all along to help me with that burden. I just needed to give it to him.

Have you ever been stuck in the efforting mode? Ever taken on the cares of the world, those trials you are facing... and taken them on yourself to carry? It sure gets heavy doesn't it? We can carry so many things... From a delayed flight to a late mortgage payment, from a broken marriage to a term paper due on Friday. A seriously ill family member, losing a job, losing a loved one... even the load of loneliness and confusion... all of us have times when we are disheartened and discouraged, sometimes to the point of "spiritually bankruptcy." I have felt that numbness before.

When I find myself "efforting," I think of Jesus' invitation to let Him take the heavy part of the yoke, leaving me the lighter side. I always envision in my mind that he takes the suitcases of burdens I am carrying, picks them up, walks by my side, and instantly I am filled with peace.

This year I have had to let go of that load daily... sometimes minute by minute. When given bad news, or walking through a tragedy with a friend, or facing a situation that seems much bigger than myself... or even facing the unknown. I have this verse up on my wall, and I claim it every day. It makes it much easier to do a victory dance, and walk in joy and faith when I am not carrying the immense load taking it on myself. It's amazing how Jesus takes those burdens and always turns them into miracles. Then I find myself asking the same question... "Why didn't I do this sooner?"

Monday, February 28, 2011

My Day in the Wheelbarrow

I wish I was an avid reader. I admire people who can just sit and read an entire book in an afternoon. Even as a little girl, I would not sit still long enough for my Mother to read books to me. I would just look at the pictures and off I would go! I am also one of those people who is a visual learner. That is why instruction manuals and I are not good friends. I think it is neat that God knows I am that way, He created me that way, and He speaks to me that way. There are so many times I wish I could paint the things He shows me in my spirit. It would be magnificent if I could get it on canvas! But instead He uses those images to help me through the journey with Him... day by day.

As I was sitting in the Dr. office today facing many unknowns... I started to feel a little anxious. We were crammed into the waiting room like sardines and I could feel that others were feeling anxious as well. Immediately God reminded me of a story that I visually have held onto for times just like these. It helps me ride faith to new limits... the new limits that go far beyond the fear of the unknown. It was just what I needed for today, and those feelings of "Oh Lord, can I handle this?"

A traveler, hiking through the wilderness, comes to the edge of a canyon. Seeking a way to the other side, he discovers a big rope stretched over the canyon. As his eyes follow the rope toward the other side, he is surprised to see a man coming toward him, confidently pushing a wheelbarrow. Arriving on his side of the canyon, the traveler exclaims, "That was truly amazing!"

The man with the wheelbarrow asks, "Do you believe that I can do it again?"

"Oh, of course," the traveler replies. "You walked across with such confidence."

"Do you really believe I can do it again?" asks the man with the wheelbarrow.

"Definitely," replies the traveler.

"Very good, then," says the man with the wheelbarrow. "Hop in and I will take you across."

Many of us look at God the same way we look at the man with the wheelbarrow. We say we have faith that God can do anything. Yet, when it comes time to get in the wheelbarrow, our faith begins to dwindle. I was sitting in the Dr. office today thinking about that very wheelbarrow. Did I have the faith to hop in? Or was my fear keeping me from the journey to the other side. God has never let me down, how could I ever doubt Him? Haven't I seen enough of His promises to trust Him to carry me across?

I started thanking God instead of doubting. I started believing that God had placed me right where I was for a reason. This was not scary, it was yet another step out of my comfort zone to trust Him like never before... that place where the miracles are. I took a deep breath and felt His presence right there with me... in the "sardine" waiting room.

Under my breath, I prayed for every person in that waiting room, and hoped they felt that peace that I was feeling. Finally after an hour wait, my name was called... I envisioned myself hopping into that wheelbarrow, and off I went, wheelbarrow and all. I knew who was pushing me after all... it was going to be a great day.

Matthew 17:20

Tuesday, March 1, 2011

My Mom's "Hair Raising" Journey...

As I drove my Mother to her hair appointment today, my mind couldn't help but go back to where I was driving exactly 1 year ago. We were on our way to the hospital...only a few feet away from where we were going for her hair appointment today. It was the beginning of one of the hardest journeys my family would ever take. I remember it like it was yesterday. I remember hearing the words I prayed I would never hear... and I was the first to hear them. "Your Mother has cancer." I felt like I was having an out of body experience... it was heart wrenching. I remember having to tell my Father. That day was the hardest day of my life. I also remember the day that my Mother lost all of her hair because of chemotherapy. It fell out on Easter, and my father shaved her head. They did it together, and her comment was... "Jesus rose today, and my hair will rise again too!" She never wavered. I never once heard my Mother utter a complaint, but I ached for her, because I knew it had to be so hard. She loved her dark hair and colored that gray the second she saw any. I always told her to let it go to her natural color. I knew she would look beautiful. She couldn't stand the thought of having gray hair. My what a year can bring. And my oh my... how perspectives and priorities can change in an instant!

As we drove together we began to talk. How precious her words are to me. She is my inspiration. She inspires me everyday and is the reason I even put my thoughts on paper... and blog. She said to me today, "Lisa, I wish I could blog, and write beautiful words of how I feel..." She went on to say "I would write about my hair. I would write about how losing my dark head of hair, and it being resurrected to the most beautiful gray frost ever... showed me God's love in ways I never dreamed." As she sat there beaming, that beautiful head of hair, styled, and so gorgeous she went on to say... "Jesus cared about my hair, Lisa, He gave me....a thicker, more beautiful head of hair!" In fact He did one better and gave me a "heavenly frost!" He walked me through my healing of cancer, and He cared about the little things as well...even my hair!" As we walked out of the hair salon, the precious lady who cut her hair said with a smile in her voice... "Do you know how much money people would pay to have that color of hair?" We smiled at each other.... yep, it's the little things.

I have to say I have never seen my Mother more happy, more beautiful, and more active in life than she is right now. We started talking about God's attention to every detail. Many times we miss those details because we are so focused on the big problems. My Mother has taught me to catch every little miracle, because sometimes they can be just as important as the big answers. And she is right! Many times in my discouragement, if I would just look a little harder, a miracle was standing right there in front of me. Little miracles like how I was protected, how God gave me favor in a situation, put me in the right place at the right time, gave me the right doctor for a surgery, and provided unexpected little financial miracles I might have overlooked if I was not looking for them. God's little miracles have even been not answering some of my prayers... His answers turned out to be better! Who'da thought! On my worst day, when I really look closely... God was there. I just had my eyes on the wrong things. My Mom has taught me to pray and expect great things with my eyes, not on my difficulties, but on God. Amazing how that changes things.

My mom's words once again, bring such joy to my soul. Every time I leave my mother from a day with her, or from a minute with her... I leave a better person. We walked through many surgeries together this year, many chemo appointments together, and many doctor's visits. Her joy permeated every second. We have laughed, cried, and prayed together harder than we ever have this year. I don't know what is ahead, but my Mother has taught me, whatever comes my way....God will take care of the big things, and the little things. My joy comes straight from His heart to mine... even on the hardest of days.

Yes, my Mother was right... as she always is. God gave her what He promised. She is walking in her healing, and this Easter she has the most beautiful head of hair again. It indeed was resurrected just as she said it would be. He paid attention to every single detail of her life... Guess you could say it was a "Hair Raising, Perspective changing" year for our family. It doesn't get better than that.

Thursday, March 10, 2011

It's Time to Dance!

As I sat listening to my favorite song from Hillsong, and as I sung the words about God's love, His power, and the beauty of His presence... I could not help but just start dancing. How could I sit still? It was impossible. So there with my dogs beside me... we danced. It wasn't pretty... oh, but it was freeing. I knew heaven was dancing with me.

I find myself dancing with praise many times throughout the day. Sometimes on my morning runs I run with my arms up in the air as I am just feeling God's freedom. In fact someone asked me the other day, out of all the hurdles this year brought, what stood out to me the most? My reply? "I learned how to dance."

To me dance is all about the heart. The heart is where the Lord engages us in an intimate exchange of love, conversation, communion and fellowship. We are drawn into His presence... He is writing in the chapters of our lives. Everyday I wake up I can hear Him saying "Lisa, will you dance with me today?"

It is so easy to get our focus on things that take us away from that presence. I heard someone say one day "It's so easy to get caught up in the ministry and get our eyes off of the Master." What can keep me close to you Lord? How can I walk through this journey of unknowns and "unexpecteds"?… I hear His voice gently reminding me... "Lisa... remember the dance." He is my eternal dance partner.

I want to be like David. He was a man after God's own heart. He danced before the Lord with all his might. He celebrated before the Lord. He habitually ran into the presence of God and his dancing resulted in amazing ministry...including killing a giant! I think that is so cool!

I am learning that my quiet time with the Lord is where my dancing shoes begin their journey. How else can I learn more about the Lead in my life if I am not spending time with Him? So this year... I learned to focus on that Lead. And an exciting adventure has been the amazing result of our dance together. I have learned that when I dance with Him I see God accomplish more than I ever dreamed for, asked for, or imagined. (Eph. 3:20) It has been through this dance that I am learning about having a heart of devotion to God and prioritizing my alone time with Him. My quiet time alone with God is at the heart of the dance with Him. It's where I engage in the most precious parts of the dance - communion, prayer, reading His word, surrender, and commitment. It is where God helps me find my purpose again. (Ever felt like you have lost your purpose?)

My greatest challenge this year in the dance has been surrendering to the Lord on those very difficult days. Those days when there are things that happen I cannot possibly wrap my mind around. And this year my life has been full of those days. I specifically remember when the Doctor told me my Mother had cancer.... I felt like I had been punched in the gut. I couldn't breathe. All I could hear was a whirring sound in my ears, and then there it was... that still small voice, my dance partner, telling me to let Him take the lead and for me to "be still and know who He was... " Psalms 46:10. I could hear Him saying to me "Lisa your precious life is a dance with me... even in this situation...we can dance." He would pick me up and dance with me, only this dance I would be in His arms. I have been in His arms a lot this year. And I have to tell you, my most amazing dances have been when I am hurting the most and I am in His arms... because I am completely surrendered to Him taking the lead.

This year I have begun to truly understand how important devotion is when it comes to the dance with my Savior and how it has led me to complete surrender. I have learned about the importance of my quiet time with Him. I have learned the importance of making decisions and resolutions from the truths I have seen in God's Word. His promises are true! He will not leave me on the dance floor alone!

As the writer of Ecclesiastes said, "There is a time... to dance." This has been one of the hardest years of my life, but I learned how to dance... that makes it the best year of my life. My time was this year... and who would have thought through one of the darkest times in my life... I learned how to dance?

It is my prayer that no matter where you are in this life... if you are in the most wonderful place, or the darkest... your dance partner awaits! Embrace, and surrender to His love and follow His lead. You will truly dance... a dance that will change your life forever.

Shall we dance?

Friday, April 1, 2011

JUMP!!!

Are you going to a foreign country, Lisa? What? I was asked this question last night not understanding quite why. But it was then that I realized a friend of mine read my post on Facebook that I was getting out of my comfort zone in a big way. She thought God was sending me to a foreign country to do missions work. As far as I know I will be here....right where I am... but on a different kind of Mission's trip. Sometimes God calls us to a place of such abandoning trust that it is as if we truly were going on a Mission's trip. Sometimes God takes us on a Mission's trip right where we are.

I picture this huge cliff in my mind... it's like jumping off into beautiful blue water... with no life raft, but having the faith God will catch you... He will be that life raft and He will take you to new places you never dreamed. He will carry you to safe ground. But think about it... how much faith would it take to really jump off? That's a huge cliff now! Do I really have faith He really would catch me? Now that's a Mission's trip!

One of my favorite verses is Jeremiah 33:3 "Call to me and I will answer you and tell you great and unsearchable things you do not know."

Not only will He catch you on your leap of faith... He will answer you... He will show you amazing things... unsearchable things you don't know! He will take you to a new place with Him!

I am realizing that this is even true for the prayers I am praying for those dear to me. Many of my precious friends are going through trials right now... heartbreaking trials... things I can't wrap my mind around. And yet at those deep times of "Really Lord?... why?" I get that indescribable peace that says... JUMP! I AM HERE LISA! And so are the answers! What I have realized more than ever is that sometimes the answer to my hardest question is... that I may never know the answer... and I am learning to be ok with that. Because where He takes me is beyond any answer to any question. He has the answer book. He IS the answer book! So I can rest and know... He's got it all figured out.

I had this conversation with my mom yesterday about those huge things in life that happen that we just don't understand... you know, those times when you feel like God forgot your address? She looked at me as said "Lisa, I don't understand so many things in my life, but what I do know is this..." And she began to sing in her sweet precious voice one of her favorite hymns:

Tho' shadows deepen, and my heart bleeds,
I will not question the way He leads;
This side of Heaven we know in part,
I will not question a broken heart.
We'll talk it over in the bye and bye
We'll talk it over, my Lord and I.
I'll ask the reasons - He'll tell me why,
When we talk it over in the bye and bye.

Tears were in her eyes as she sang. I began to listen to her sweet voice singing and it was as if Jesus was right there with her singing along. She had jumped off the cliff and was resting in His arms. Her journey had brought her to that cliff many times this year. She didn't have answers, Jesus was all she needed. Her life has been a living testimony of that to me. She lives everyday in His arms.

So am I taking a Missions trip? Yep! Right over a big ole' cliff! The things I don't understand, the trials and hurdles that seem so insurmountable, all the questions... I leave behind. I trust the future and the answers to the one who has the big life raft waiting... His arms are big... and they are about ready to catch me! Wanna join me? Let's go for a JUMP! It's gonna be a life changer! Yahoo!

Tuesday, April 12, 2011

"Yes Lord, I'll Trust You…"

Will you trust me, Lisa? I heard that voice as I stood in the kitchen making coffee. Will you trust me? Really trust me? I knew that when I was asked twice... I better trust... and hang on. Sure enough that night as I sat up in my bed just hearing the news from Jordan, I didn't even know how respond. Shock? Anger? Disbelief? Overwhelmed. It's one thing to have faith for a situation in my own life, but when the enemy hits my kids... whoa... .that's a whole different ballgame. Will you trust me Lisa?....there it was again. Sigh... "Yes Lord, I trust you".

Jordan was getting ready to go back to Nashville after a wonderful Spring Break...only to find out that his apartment at school was burglarized. They took everything. Computers, cameras, all his guitars and sound equipment… they even took clothes. All his portfolios, all his books... even the childhood bible that had chapel notes and church notes from his life... gone. "Will you trust me Lisa?... yes Lord, I will".

I was finding that the journey of the past months and the struggles in my health were a piece of cake to trust for.... but when it came to seeing my children suffer, being under attack...the trust came harder. I kept taking back the worry. As a mom, I spend hours a day praying for my children. I want to hang onto them for dear life. But as they grow older and are now adults... the complete release of them to the Lord is a necessary journey. I released their lives and dedicated them to Jesus when they were babies... He carried them their entire lives... He never let them go... He never will. I just have to trust. I was learning to let go in a deeper way than I ever had.

And just as I was tempted to pick up the worry about just hearing the news from Jordan...that still small trusting voice just said...."Watch Lisa....watch!" So I did. And you know what I saw? I saw my son run to the Lord. In a situation that was quite devastating... he didn't cry, he didn't yell, he didn't get angry... he quietly turned around and went upstairs... and he prayed. He trusted God... with it all. "Do you trust me Lisa?" Yes Lord... I trust you! God had begun the answer from the very start... inside my son. As a mother, there are no words that describe the joy in your heart when you see your child walk out their love and trust for Jesus... even in the middle of a storm.

We decided to move Jordan back from Nashville so he could regroup, reorganize, and get enrolled in another school here at home. We can't even count the miracles God has done for Jordan this week. Far beyond what we ever dreamed. He is restoring bigger and better! We have seen Romans 8:28 come to pass! All things have truly worked together for our good! "Will you trust me Lisa?"

As I sit here, up early this morning... the house is quiet. I am filled with reflections of the year. It's been a year of many hurdles... many trials and journeys that seem insurmountable at times. But I smile inside, because you know what? God showed up in ways I never dreamed. Many times He lifted me over the hurdles, other times He jumped them with me. Some times He coached me through them, while cheering me on. When it came to my children... He held them in His arms... as tightly as a mother does with her newborn child... and He walked them ever protected over the hurdles from the attacks of the enemy... in those everlasting, strong arms.

I have learned this year just how big those arms really are. They hold my family, they hold my future, they hold my hopes and dreams, they hold it all. They hold the knowing that He is with me every second, through every question, and every hurt. I never want to leave those everlasting arms... "Yes, Lord... I trust you... with every hurdle, Lord.... I trust you."

Friday, April 22, 2011

A Song Sung From Heaven …

As my eyes were closed, just in the beginning stages of awakening today... I could hear in my spirit her sweet sweet voice as it cracked. I could see the straight pins in her collar where she kept them while she sewed clothes for homeless children. I saw the precious face of my Grandma... and as she rocked in her rocking chair, sewing away, and singing... the melody rang out and it was oh so beautiful.

On a hill far away stood an old rugged cross,
The emblem of suff'ring and shame;
And I love that old cross where the dearest and best
For a world of lost sinners was slain:
So I'll cherish the old rugged cross,
Till my trophies at last I lay down;
I will cling to the old rugged cross,
And exchange it some day for a crown.

I always could tell this song came straight from her soul. I would always watch my Grandma as she hummed and sang this song... wondering what it was about that song that meant so much to her. She never could make it to the end without tears streaming down her face.

As I awakened this morning I felt covered with such a peaceful presence. That peaceful presence that has carried me everyday through some really tough stuff this year. The peace that was there when I saw my Mom suffering through cancer... the peace that was there when my health failed and I had to trust with everything in me that He knew what He was doing and had a beautiful plan... the peace that is there when I see my friends hurting so deeply and I can't fix it... but He can. The peace that is there when the enemy comes at my children and I am helpless... and in complete surrender... to trust Him with their lives. (Oh how hard that is sometimes...) but then His peace comes... and I know I can do it. The peace that carries me when I just cannot take one more step. It was then that I realized that my Grandma, through the many trials in her life and all she endured, never wavered in her passion for her Savior. She knew this peace... she heard His voice, and His presence lived within her every day of her life. Not only did she believe the words to that song... it was her life.

I remember the day that the song "Jesus Loves Me" really soaked in. I mean REALLY soaked in. He loves ME! And the love I felt washed over my soul. I can never sing that song now without crying. Although I had heard it a million times... this one day... it changed my life. Well today... the "Old Rugged Cross" has had the same effect. As I heard the serenade from heaven... my Grandma's sweet voice... I realized that old rugged cross meant more to me than ever. Because He died for me on that cross, because of this day... I made it with Him through it all this year. His presence was there because of that old rugged cross. I cannot even fathom what Jesus went through... it has taken on a whole new meaning for me this year. Somehow, I know my Grandma knew all along... I would one day be right where she was, and I would walk out one of the hardest years of my life... right by His side. And I would be singing this song under my breath. And just as she did... I would be wiping the tears when I was done. It would come straight from my soul just as it came from hers.

In that old rugged cross, stained with blood so divine,
A wondrous beauty I see,
For 'twas on that old cross Jesus suffered and died,
To pardon and sanctify me.
To the old rugged cross I will ever be true;
Its shame and reproach gladly bear;
Then He'll call me some day to my home far away,
Where His glory forever I'll share.

Tuesday, May 3, 2011

A Life Lesson… From My Dogs

I have learned so much from my dogs. Yeah I know… sounds funny huh? For all you dog lovers out there, you know what I mean. I wasn't always as much of a dog person as I am today. My dogs are a joy to my heart. When my kids left the nest, we filled them with dogs! My wonderful husband is so accommodating and so supportive of my love for my dogs, and has become just as attached to them as I have.

Today I took them all on a walk in the beautiful sunshine. It is my prayer time and my alone time with God. I always ask God to teach me something each day… to find hidden treasures even in the midst of trials that come. (And there seem to have been many hurdles this year.) I guess that is why there have been many lessons. I treasure those lessons. But today it was a simple lesson. It was about friendship. It was about how I love my family, and my husband. And who would have thought I would have learned it from my dogs?

Our golden retriever, Gracie-Anne is her own adjective. If I ever figure it out, I'll let you know. Her energy is endless. She's a gift giver. She never comes empty handed… (or mouthed) She is a child at heart and quite frankly I don't think she will ever grow up. Her excitement is genuine and to the core. (Or should I say over-excitement!) She has her quirks, like eating anything… and I mean ANYTHING in sight. How many trips to the vet have we taken with her? Too many to count. But her innocence and sweet heart make those trips worth it. She just gets so excited that she swallows the gifts she brings you! Now that's excitement!

Then there's my Holly, our lab. My sweet Holly who was trained to be a service dog, but bless her heart, her hips didn't want to cooperate so she stayed with me. She is a service dog at heart. It is written in her face and expressed through her tail that can whip a hole in a wall at one swipe! And those of you who know Holly are nodding their heads. I have never met a sweeter soul than Holly. She is always there. No matter where I am… she is there. If I start to trip and fall, she is there in front of me bracing to catch my fall. If I drop something, she picks it up mid air and gives it back to me. As I struggled in my health this year… Holly knew. It was written all over her face, and her closeness grew even closer. She has even licked tears from my face. Holly would die for me. In fact one day on our morning run, we were faced with 2 dogs who got loose and were on the attack… straight for us. They were pit bulls who were on their way to the pound and got loose. They were fighting dogs (which made me sad) I found out later, and had dug themselves out from the fenced area. Well you can imagine what I was feeling as

I saw these 2 salivating dogs coming straight at us! I saw my life flash before my eyes... and I just froze. I knew I had no way out of this one. But Holly braced herself in front of me like a cement wall protecting me, no growling, no moving... .just protecting. I will never ever forget the look on her face. It was like she knew what was about to happen, but she had peace. She knew it would be ok. And in one of my previous blogs you will see what happened next. God protected... and Holly was my angel that day. It was a miracle. Holly is steadfast, unconditionally loving, and immovable in her love. In fact I would go as far to say she is one of the most passionate dogs I have ever seen.

And then there is Mavis. Oh Mavis. Mavis Pearl is our newest addition and she is bulldog to the core. I am watching her personality unfold daily and she is a hoot! But what bull dog isn't? Mavis has a sense of humor that makes you laugh until you collapse. Just watching her walk is fun! Training Mavis is not like training a golden or a lab. She has learned so much already, but is not treat motivated. (Motivation is not her strength) She trains by affection! She'd much rather have a "YES!" and a hug, than a treat. In fact the treat will stay on the floor and she will be looking up at me with that wrinkled smushed in face as if to say... "Oh just say YES, and good girl please!!" Since she is too fat to snuggle, she gets as close to me as she can and vibrates (her way of breathing.) She is a stubborn girl at times, and loves to eat my shoes. My new high heeled shoes I bought for Easter are now flats with missing bows. Oh well, I can't walk in heels anyway. She's her own personality. She knows no personal boundaries and gets right in your face. Holly and Gracie don't like her lack of personal space boundaries, and have called her on it often. She's learning.

So as I walked this morning with the 3 of them, thinking about their individual traits, I thought to myself.... what kind of a friend am I? What traits do I have and share with others? What kind of a Mom and wife am I? Am I giver, a kid at heart? Do I love unconditionally and have passion? Am I stubborn and relentless? Am I steadfast and always there to show God's love? Am I a protector and peacemaker? Do I have boundaries? It made me reflect on the kind of person I am and the kind of person I want to be. I have so far to go, but know God is constantly on this journey with me refining me. Just as a little puppy can be trained to become a service dog one day and change lives.. .God is constantly training and refining me and completing what He has begun. Some days are not as fun as others, but the lessons learned are life-changing. I want to become more like Him everyday. It's a journey. A journey He will take straight to His heart. He will never leave or forsake me on this journey. He loves me when I fall, He loves me when I succeed. He loves me... period.

Isn't that just the neatest thing ever? Yep, it was a great walk with my 3 buddies this morning. I learned a lot from them today... I am thankful. It's going to be a great day!

Philippians 1:6: For I am confident of this very thing, that He who began a good work in you will perfect it until the day of Christ Jesus.

Friday, May 6, 2011

God's Heart for Single Moms … Happy Mother's Day

It happened as I was cleaning the house today. A vivid memory I had not thought about in years. But today for some reason it came out of nowhere. There I was, in the 3rd row of the sanctuary at church, I was holding my baby boy, and my 2 year old daughter was sitting to my side. It was Mother's day. I was wiping the tears away as fast as they they came. I tried to hide them, but it was impossible. It was overwhelming. How would I do it? How could I raise these children by myself? It was our first Mother's Day together with my babies, alone. How could this happen? How was I left to do this by myself? It was the first time it really hit me. I was on this journey now with just Jesus, and my babies. And it was also at that time that my life changed forever. My relationship with Jesus went to a whole new level. He was the lover of my soul, my husband, my maker, my friend... He was my everything. And by His grace He walked me through one of the most difficult times of my life... being a single mom.

Today as I was cleaning, thinking about Mother's Day, my heart felt such a burden... a burden to pray... to pray for those single Mom's out there who are single for whatever reason, yet are giving their all to raise their children. I remember that time... I remember that feeling of loneliness... the feeling that you just couldn't do it another day. I remember wondering if God had forgotten where I lived, how did this happen to me? My self esteem was shattered. How would He put the pieces back together again? Could He? Would He? Would my children be ok? Did God forget those deep desires of my heart to be a wife AND mom? Mother's Day... took on a whole new meaning for me.

As I was praying and cleaning and wondering why Jesus was taking me down this journey today, it was then that I looked at the picture on the desk... there it was... the joys of my life. My 4 kids, 3 dogs, and my wonderful husband. My favorite picture daily reminding me of the miracle God performed. Not only did Got not forget the deepest desires of my heart, He brought those dreams into fruition far greater than I ever dreamed. I held that picture to my heart today, and the tears started flowing. I thought about the past 10 years with a husband I utterly adore, and 4 children who all love Jesus passionately who are the joys of my life, and I realize once again... just how amazing God's grace truly is. He gave me the deepest desires of my heart. He saw those tears and heard the cries of my heart that Sunday morning years ago. He knew the journey would be amazing. He held my hand and He walked me through every step.

There is hope! There is restoration! There is grace! There are miracles! My heart this Mother's Day is with all of you single Mother's out there who are weary, who are overwhelmed, who are wanting to give up, who are lonely, and feeling forgotten. Oh friend, Jesus wants to take you to a whole new place. This journey that seems to be an endless, thankless one is indeed a journey straight to His heart. He utterly adores you! He sees every tear you have cried, He hears the cries of your heart. He hears! I pray this Mother's day you are engulfed in the arms of the lover of your soul... Jesus. I felt those arms in ways that carried me through the darkest of days. I also want you to know I am praying for you. I want to encourage you! Hang on to those dreams you have. Hold on tight! He will bring them to pass in your life in ways you cannot even imagine. (Eph 3:20)

Mothers are very dear to the Lord... precious indeed. My prayer is that this Mother's day you get a glimpse of the treasure you truly are! May this Mother's day mark the beginning of your miracle journey! I promise, you will look back on this journey, and you will smile at the miracles God walked you through. Get ready! The best is yet to come!

Happy Mother's Day!

Sunday, May 15, 2011

To Have a Pity Party, or Not Have a Pity Party... That is the Question!

As my eyes began to open from a restless sleep... I could tell this one would be tough. My mind was telling my body to "Move!" "Get up!" but it wouldn't budge. For those of you who struggle with an autoimmune issue such as spondyloarthritis... or any kind of arthritis for that matter... you know what I am talking about. Mornings can be tough. The mind is ready to go... the body, quite a different story. And it can be different everyday.

So as I was lying there I thought to myself....this is a grand opportunity for a pity party! Balloons and all! Then there it was... that precious still small voice of the Holy Spirit behind the wailing pity party horns, calling me. Yep, there it was... sweetly whispering to me to replace those party horns for something much better. He told me to start thanking Him. Be grateful! It was not just an "attitudinal change" He was calling me into, but a "gratitudinal change." Are you kidding me Lord? My joints are swollen, my body is screaming with pain... I am discouraged!... HOW? "Just listen Lisa....start thanking... you'll see." I would put Him to the test! So I started praising through the pain. If I told you it was easy I would be lying. My pillow was soaked with tears, but I began my journey to praise no matter what. I began to realize as I sat there crying, praying and thanking... that being grateful was the beginning of something so much deeper. He wanted me to live in the fullness of my relationship with Him, not hindered and hamstrung and holding Him at arm's length, but experiencing Him richly... feeling at home in His presence. It was then that I realized He did not want me to be destroyed by the inevitable downturns of life, with no answer for the darts of unfair, unpleasant circumstances... a walking bull's eye, just waiting for the next arrow to be shot in my direction. He wanted me to find the God given reserve to stand strong in the midst of confusing, condemning onslaughts of opposition and pain. He wanted my head up, lifted by the empowering Spirit of God within me, even when everything else within me was calling me for a day in bed with the lights out and the blinds drawn and pity party horns blaring. He was calling me to "gratitudinal change"... and He wanted me to be a person who's known and marked by gratitude. I could not do it in my own strength. But I could do it through His strength. He took me from my weakest point, and began to work. I just had to let go, let Him, and start thanking.

You know what I realized? At first...thanking God in the pain was difficult... but as I released and kept on thanking... I felt it began to lift. I felt a change in perspective. I went from seeing things through my pity party colored glasses to seeing them through gratitude colored glasses. I saw the pain and problems that usually buried me take a back seat. Those problems took their rightful place BEHIND twenty other blessings that were bigger than those problems would ever be. A recurring issue that once brought out a whole range of pent up emotions was now producing a new excuse to praise God with greater fervor than ever. I knew He was more than trustworthy. Gratitude was changing things.

You know what else I have learned through this journey today? God loves me. His promises are sure, and my heavenly destiny is settled forever through Jesus. But some of His work in me and through me can only come through the valley of shadow and suffering. Was I going to be resistant to it? Or was I going to be clay in His hands knowing He is intent on shaping my life for something far bigger than my own comfort, convenience and pleasure. I could surrender, or go kicking and screaming... pity party and all.

I chose surrender! I took my pity party hat off, shut the party horns down, and chose today to make gratitude my default setting. And you know what... it worked. Not only was my day blessed with His presence, but my body was too. And my faith was renewed to know that He was my healer and would take care of it all, even on the days when my body was telling me otherwise. Again, I knew He was on this amazing journey with me... and He would not let me down. I love my gratitude colored glasses. I pray you get some too! They beat pity party glasses any day!

I challenge you to make gratitude your default setting today, and see what happens!
See you in your new glasses!

Wednesday, May 18, 2011

God, Betty Crocker and Chili Powder?

As I sat there anxiously waiting, staring at my wonderful masterpiece in the oven to be finished, I was so excited! My first try at a new cake recipe (gluten free, sugar free) and I was feelin' like Chef Lisa with my huge oven mitts on. I just needed the hat! I was in between appointments, but I was craving something sweet! So as fast as I could, I was pouring the ingredients into the bowl, and determined I would have my cake within the hour.

I heard the buzzer ring, and you would have thought it was the finish line in a race. I sprinted! It was beautiful! I was so proud! I love to bake, but my skills as a gluten free pastry chef are severely lacking. The gluten free journey I am now walking through is a new one. But I am determined to make the best of it, by golly!

The house was quiet, and I was all alone, which is rare these days. Just my dogs staring up at me sensing my "cake excitement!" As I sliced my first piece (yes, I knew there would be a second) I almost wanted to sing the hallelujah chorus! This was my first taste of anything sweet in 2 months. Can you tell? I took my first bite, knowing how amazing it would be... and my mouth came to a screeching halt! It was HORRIBLE! What kind of recipe was this? I knew it could not have been my baking skills! Surely I was not that bad of a cook! I re-traced my steps, and all of the sudden (not wanting to admit that I am literally blind without my reading glasses) I realized that instead of cinnamon, I put in chili powder. And are you ready for this... I left out the sugar! (or Stevia powder in this case, since I can't have sugar.) There it was sitting in the measuring cup, and right in front of me (which I realized after I put on my glasses) I felt like such a dork! Seriously Lisa? Chili powder? Fail!

Totally bummed, I threw the cake in the sink and mumbled under my breath... "Well this was a waste of time." But you know what is so funny, under my mumbling breath I heard the Lord say "Maybe to you, but not to me." "What Lord?" I say that often these days... in amazement at what He is telling and teaching me. It was then that I began to see the lesson He was wanting to teach me from my cake disaster.

Many times in my impatience of "Hurry up Lord!"... I see that it's like He's baking a cake! Yep... being the visual person that I am, I saw cake! All the wonderful ingredients (gifts) in my life are delicately being put together. It's measured perfectly, and it is not done hurriedly. (and He has 20/20 vision and no reading glasses!) He knows what it takes for a perfect recipe. He knows just how long it takes for the cake to bake... but it has to bake. That means heat! Refinement! God has the ingredients together, and now the refinement. Some things are made beautiful by the heating process. In this case as He was showing me... He was working out the things in my life perfectly, some were in the oven... the desert... the dry land... the dark place (the oven!) But what comes out is a wonderful masterpiece! In that masterpiece come the answers, the healing, the miracles!

This put things into a whole new perspective. I knew these things in my heart, but today it just hit home. In fact His whole journey for me these past two years have been a journey of realizations. Things I was taught, knew, and learned my entire life have begun to become a part of who I am. I was living them, not just learning them. Instead of hearing about God's baking abilities, I was watching Him bake... and it was my life he was baking! I have to admit, as I sat there reflecting on all of this I thought about Shadrach, Meshach and Abednego and the fiery furnace (Daniel, Ch.3) What a devotion to God they had! God really did spectacular things in that oven! Wow! Now that's an oven story!

Yes Lord, I guess you did have something to teach me today after all. I will leave the baking to you! Off goes the oven mitt, and my ideas of being the gluten free Betty Crocker. I know God blows Betty Crocker out of the water anyway, and I know the cake He is baking will be unique, and complete in every way. It will be topped with a frosting of miracles, and healing, and it will be delightful! It is my job to give Him the chef's hat, and leave the baking to him. After all who wants chili powder in a cake!

I think I'll go to Whole Foods and get a fruit smoothie! Bon Appétit!

Monday, May 23, 2011

Clara's Pot Roast

 When Clara entered the room, you knew she was there. She had a raspy voice and profanities flew out everywhere. She was loud, and she was abrupt. She was the cleaning lady that worked for the apartment complex I was managing years ago. She was rough around the edges, but boy could she clean! Her hard life showed on her face. The abuse she had endured for years had taken its toll, and it was apparent, she would not let anyone hurt her. Her guard was always up. She worked tirelessly to raise her teenage son, and she was devoted to him. Her husband left her, and she was alone. Her life was her son. Everyone tried to steer clear of Clara, but I always had such a soft place in my heart for her. She would always end up in my office, challenging me about this so called "Jesus" I served. She loved to talk about how she would never become a Christian. She thought Christians were fake, mean, and full of deceit. I always prayed for Clara, everyday, and I always asked the Lord to show me how to lead her to Him... what could I say? His response to me was always... "Don't say anything Lisa... just love her." She was a hard person to love on some days, but at the end of the day, she always ended up talking to me about her life. Some days her pain was so evident.

I will never forget when I got the phone call. On the other end of the line was a family member of Clara's explaining to me that Clara's son had just been killed in a car wreck. It was a horrific accident. My heart sank. In fact I remember sitting there for about an hour after I hung up the phone just staring at the wall, praying. What should I do? What could I do? What words could be said? I spent that sleepless night praying for Clara, and as I kept asking the Lord what to do, I so clearly heard in my heart... "Make pot roast!" Yes, I know... comedy at a time like this? "Lord, seriously... what can I do?" And again, I heard.. ."Make pot roast!" Hmmm, now this was a first for me in many areas. I had never heard the Lord tell me to make pot roast, and I had never even made pot roast!!! Really?

I got up early the next morning, and I went to the store and I bought 4 of the biggest pot roasts I could find with all the trimmings. This was going to be interesting to say the least! For a solid day, I made pot roast. I found my Grandma's recipe, and I prayed over those pot roasts and dove in! If there ever was going to be an anointed pot roast this would be it!

Thinking that the Lord was going to give me some eloquent words for this family as I brought them pot roast, I approached the front door. Clara opened the door... just as I asked the Lord to give me the words, and as quickly as He said "pot roast", was as quickly as He said... "Lisa, don't say a word." Clara took the pot roasts from my arms, sat them down and grabbed me. She held me for what seemed like an eternity, and she cried from a part of her soul that I could tell had never been reached before. I also felt those cries shoot right up to heaven. Jesus loved Clara so much... Jesus had a plan for Clara, and pot roast would only be the seed planted to begin His mighty work.

My words were few to Clara that day... there were mostly just tears. A lot of tears. I did look over Clara's shoulder and see a room full of people diving into the pot roast, and I saw the look on their faces. I felt so helpless to know what to do or say at such a heartbreaking time like this. So I just prayed. I prayed that God would work a miracle for this family. All I could do was plant a small seed.

And boy did pot roast seem so small to me in light of such a huge tragedy.

Clara never came back to clean after her son died. In fact I didn't even see Clara again after that day. I always prayed for Clara, and always wondered what happened to her. Would I ever know?

I was checking my emails one morning, and there was one that stood out to me. It was from "Pot Roast Clara". What? Was this a virus? I laughed, but by the time I finished the letter... my laughs were tears streaming down my face. It was Clara! My cleaning lady Clara! But she was no longer a cleaning lady.

She worked (are you ready for this?) at a church where she prepared meals for home bound people, and people who were ill in the church. Her specialty? Pot Roast! (Thus the name Pot Roast Clara!)

As Clara and I emailed and talked back and forth over the next few weeks I cannot tell you how my life changed. What I felt was such an insignificant seed planted that day, changed a life. God did the watering through others, through leaders, through events He orchestrated... and she came to Jesus in a way I cannot even describe. I asked her what changed her life? Her voice began to crack and she said... "It was the pot roast." She went on to say that it was what was "not spoken" to her on that day that changed her entire thinking about Jesus.

She said "Lisa, you were the only one who came, you were the only one who made a meal, you were the only one who didn't preach to us with big words. You were just there, and you loved us just the way we were, curse words and all. She went on to say that it was one day as she was eating a sandwich made out of the pot roast... she accepted the Lord into her heart. She said it was quiet, it was sweet, and it was real. And bless her heart, she said she never uttered a word of profanity after that roast beef sandwich!

At this point I am in one of those "ugly cries"... you know the kind you can't breathe and stuff is running out your nose, eyes and mouth... it isn't pretty. Oh, but it felt so good! I remember those days when I felt Clara was unreachable... but God didn't!

That day changed my thinking. I realized that every seed I planted mattered. No seed was too small. I may not see the harvest, but God was busy watering the seed, and that seed would grow! Just because I may not see the harvest didn't mean it wasn't there!

I also learned that day that it wasn't many times my words that would lead others to Him, it was what I didn't say. It was what I lived. One of my favorite quotes is

"We are told to let our light shine, and if it does, we won't need to tell anybody it does. Lighthouses don't fire cannons to call attention to their shining – they just shine."

When I think about it, some of the times I have been touched the most have been when I have watched a person live out loud, and love out loud. Loving out loud may begin with the smallest seed... a hug, a smile, shared time... but what ends up is a miracle! The harvest! A symphony! And sometimes even a pot roast!

Happy seed planting!
Galatians 6:9

Sunday, May 29, 2011

Free to be Authentic and Mask Free!

As I walked into the cafe, I heard laughter. Focused on getting in and out with my juice I didn't pay much attention. That is until I looked up and realized they were pointing and laughing at me! Uh oh... what did I have hanging out of my nose? Was there toilet paper on my shoe? Did my shoes not match... again? Was my zipper unzipped? What could be so funny? My first thought was get in the car and go somewhere else. But I was too far in the cafe, so I walked past them as fast as I could and stood in line for my juice. I could feel my heart racing all the way up to my nostrils thinking that something had to be wrong with me! Why were they pointing and laughing? All I wanted was a juice!

As I stood there trying to figure it all out... my mind went back to a conversation I had with one of my daughters recently. It was about authenticity. It was about being real. It was about showing who we really are and not being afraid to shine for God in confidence. It's about not caring what the world thinks, it's about what God thinks. It's about knowing who we are in Christ, and not walking in fear, but in confidence. It was about walking without a mask on so that others could see our authenticity.

Authenticity? What does that really even mean anyway?

I remember doing a study with my daughter and we looked up the word authenticity. This is what we found: Authenticity: loyalty, faithfulness, sincerity, devotion, honesty, steadfastness, fidelity, safety, security, reliable, firm, unimpeachable, real, not copied or duplicated. Now that's a pretty amazing word isn't it? Wow! I want to be authentic!!!

We had such a special time that day and prayed that God would help us walk in authenticity! Not walking in fear, but in confidence of who we were! We even wrote out the definition and put it up to see.

Then all of the sudden, waiting for my juice...I realized how the enemy uses such trivial things to trip us up, to lose sight of the authenticity God wants us to walk in. The enemy is always there with a counterfeit lie to cause us confusion. Have you ever listened to those lies? "You are not good enough, not pretty enough, not smart enough, not thin enough, not spiritual enough, just not enough!" Oh I have! There are days I wake up and it's roaring like a lion in my ears! But always behind those roars, is that still small voice of the Holy Spirit reminding me of my authenticity. Who I am in Him! Will I listen to the roars? Or will I listen to the still small voice?

I began to chuckle as I stood in line... how funny was this!!!! I was listening to the roars that something was wrong with me, when I knew who I was... why fear? What would the authentic Lisa do? I would go out there, say hello to that table of laughing people, and be friendly! Seriously? Yep, that's what I would do. Easier said than done right?

I proceeded to get my juice, and also bought some gluten free cookies on the way out. I was my authentic self by golly and I was on a mission! I went out the same door I came in and there they were, still at their table... the laughing ladies! Oh my. I walked over (yes, feeling my heartbeat in my nostrils still) and placed the cookies on the table. A look of surprise came over their faces, as I said "Hello!" I asked them if they would like some cookies with their coffee, and they were delighted! Was this the same table of people? Yes, it was! I struck up a conversation with them and come to find out, they were there meeting about gluten free recipes, and food! NO WAY! They all get together every now and then to support each other. If you know my story, you know I have to eat gluten free because of celiac disease, and so does my son. I had just said recently to a friend of mine... "I just need help! I don't know how to be creative with all of this gluten free cooking!" And there before me were piles of recipes and friends to help me! I am so glad I did not miss this opportunity!

And for you who are wondering why they were laughing at me... I asked them that very question! You know what is funny? They were not laughing at me at all! They were telling funny stories and didn't even know they had pointed or laughed! Really? I bought into the lie I was the brunt of their jokes? They thought it was so funny that I thought they were laughing at me! Wow! I was about to put on my mask and hide, feeling rejected. I am so thankful I threw the mask to the wind and grabbed the gluten free cookies instead! Thank you still small voice... you have never failed me!

I realize more than ever that God has His hand on me every second. He wants to answer my prayers! It is my choice, and my will that many time divert His will. It is my choice to listen to the lies, or listen to the truth. It is my choice to leave the mask at home, or take it with me. Better yet, not even own one!

Have you ever worn a real mask before? It is hot, it gets smelly in there after awhile, and it's not comfortable. Kind of like wearing the mask of someone you really are not. It's a smelly, uncomfortable process after awhile! One of my favorite quotes is from Rick Warren: "The most exhausting activity is pretending. Faking is fatiguing. Duplicity creates anxiety. Wearing a mask wears you out."

Authenticity! That has become my new favorite word! There's such freedom in being authentic! I want it to become a part of who I am. Oh the wonderful things that await when the mask is taken off! I hope you will walk with me in this process, and love who you are! God sure does! In fact He is up there dancing over you with singing at the very thought of you! (Zeph. 3:17)

That just makes me want to dance a jig! A mask free jig! Care to join me?

Sunday, June 5, 2011

The Eyes Truly Are the Window to a Soul… What's in Your Window?

As I stepped out of the van, I was immediately pulled out by one of the helpers to come down to the basement where they housed the food pantry for the homeless. "It was an emergency", he said, and my arm was the first one he grabbed to help. What was going on? I was in the middle of our Music Ministry Tour with my ORU Music team many years ago. and we were ministering in the Bronx, NY. It was in the worst part of town, and we would be there for a few days. Little did I know God was about to put the Bronx forever in my heart. Things were about to change, really fast!

As I was taken downstairs, the staff director said to me, "She's been beaten again, this time with a baseball bat. She was hit so hard, they found the bat broken in two pieces. We don't know how long or if she will even make it. The E.R. probably won't come because this happens weekly to her. She was homeless. Just stay with her OK?" OK? What was I walking into? Why was I the one chosen? God... HELP!

It was all a blur until I saw her. There she was on the floor in the fetal position, blood everywhere, so thin, so frail, her hair falling out, some of her nails missing, bruises everywhere. She was bleeding internally. I could not even find a patch of skin that was not purple. I remember uttering out loud, but my voice not making it out... "Oh Jesus, I need you... oh how I need you." Immediately a warm rush flooded my body and I knew the Holy Spirit was right there with me. I instantly felt calm. That empty cold basement with one chair that was now filled with just me and this precious woman... was instantly filled with His presence. I picked her up, and put her in my arms. I sat in the creaking rocking chair with her, and I rocked. I found out later her name was Sarah. She was not conscious. Where were the people? Where was the help? Why wouldn't they help her? I didn't know the answers, I didn't need to. God knew. So I just rocked. That picture to this day is forever etched into my mind and heart.

What was I supposed to do now? I heard the Lord whisper in my heart. "Sing over her, pray over her, love her with your heart, let me do the rest." Your eyes are the window to your soul, and she will see." How could she see? She was unconscious!

So I sang. I sang Jesus Loves Me, I sang songs my Grandma and Mom would sing over me when I was hurting, I sang songs we were singing on this tour, I sang about heaven, I sang about healing. I sang prayers of healing over her. I just sang. At one point I thought she had passed away, but I saw her little finger move. I kept singing. As I sang I felt a presence of the Lord like never before. He was there in that room, helping me hold on for this dear lady. She may not have mattered to anyone, she may not have had family, she may have been homeless for years and had nobody, but she mattered to Jesus. She mattered so much to Him that He was holding her in His arms, and God chose me to be those arms for Him... and He was holding me as I held onto her! After 4 hours of singing, and what little voice I had left... still singing... I saw her eyelashes flutter. I saw a deep purple in her body which they said was internal bleeding, begin to lighten. I felt her skin begin to change temperature. I sang and I prayed "Oh

Jesus! please heal her, please give her purpose, please be her Savior and save her!" To this day I don't think I have cried out like that ever. It was pure desperation! God knew. God heard. She ever so gently reached over and grabbed my finger. She squeezed it with a gentle squeeze. It was like she was holding on with whatever bit of life she had left. Would I be the last person she would see? I just held and kept singing, wiping my own tears at this point.

I missed the concert that night. I was in the basement holding this sweet lady. My songs on this night would be sung to one, not hundreds. After 4 more hours, her eyes opened. They were crystal blue. I remember through all the broken blood vessels, that beautiful blue. They looked up at me and there it was. A beautiful smile! She was missing most of her teeth, but it was the most beautiful smile I'd ever seen. For the next hour she watched me as I sang, I never talked to her... I just sang. At one point I stopped, just looked into her eyes, and asked the Lord to speak everything He wanted her to hear, through my eyes, not saying a word. It was the only way I could communicate to her at that moment... He answered.

There was a knock on the door, and an E.R. tech was there. He was expecting to come to pick up her body. By then, her color was pink, her eyes were clearing, and she was sitting up drinking some water. All I remember was the look on his face of sheer shock, and him uttering the words... "Are you kidding?" Nope, I was not kidding, and neither was the Lord. He took this very seriously.

In fact He took it so seriously that a precious family in the church took this lady in. They paid for her medical bills and took her to the hospital. They were so touched by the miracle of her life, and her story and knew God had plans for her. I will never forget this family ever. Angels sent from heaven, and answers to my prayers for this lady. Before we left for our next stop, the family found me and had news to share. They told me that when they began talking with Sarah after she became completely conscious, they asked her what she needed or wanted. Her reply was "I want what the lady singing to me had in her eyes." The family told me they prayed over her, and she accepted the Lord that day. They said it was a precious time. As they told me this story, I fell to my knees, literally. I began to sob. I didn't even have words. What a mighty God I served! I just cried and hugged this family. I was so thankful for them.

I lost touch with that family but the last communication I had with them, Sarah was doing great! She was regaining her health. She was involved in a support group at the church that helped battered women and she loved singing in the choir. They said Sarah's passion was to sing! She glowed when she sang. They said that singing gave her purpose. Sarah found her purpose! She was a praiser! Oh I knew God had big plans for Sarah. I write about this story with tears streaming down my face. Sarah changed my life that day I held her in my arms. I learned that we hold heaven in our eyes, we hold healing in our spirit, we hold life in the darkness when we can't say a word at all. God uses it all, and makes miracles happen even when there are no words involved.

I have learned that some of the most life changing speeches, have no words at all. They can touch the untouchable, reach the unreachable, love the unlovable... they can touch a hurting world for Him.

There was a song that we sung on tour called "Heaven in Your Eyes" by Jeremy Dalton. It was a duet that I sang with my dear friend on tour. From that day on, I could never get through the song without getting choked up. The words became a reality to me the day I held Sarah in my arms. I would never be the same.

We are mirrors... what do we reflect? What shines out when we look at those who are hurting. Do we have heaven to offer? When others look at us, what will they find? We can change the world without saying a word. We can live out loud and not utter a sound. How very true it is......

Love never fails. Never. Just ask Sarah.

Friday, June 10, 2011

Heavenly Interruptions

Have you ever had a song stuck in your head and it played and played over in your mind throughout the day? Well yesterday I was singing "Raindrops on roses and whiskers on kittens, bright copper kettles and warm woolen mittens... brown paper packages tied up with string".... and you know the rest. Yes, Julie Andrews and the Von Trapp family were filling my mind with the song about "favorite things." I don't know why it was in my mind, but it made me start thinking about my favorite things. What put a smile on my face? What brought me delight?

Depending on what season of life you are in, your source of delight may vary. "Delight" simply describes something that provokes in you a pleasurable emotion, a sense of deep enjoyment or a high degree of satisfaction. Daily delights are all around us, if we only look. We many times forget that God will use what we take delight in to accomplish His will.

I was talking with a lady not long ago who felt she could only hear God's voice in the desert, in the dark times. She struggled to hear Him on her day to day journey. At times she felt like He was not even there. She was feeling so discouraged.

Many people assume that an encounter with God can only be experienced through pain and suffering. But there is good news! While trials do teach Christians a great deal, they are not the only catalysts God uses to accomplish His will in our lives! If I have learned nothing else in these past 3 years of walking through my Mother's cancer journey and through my own health journey it is that God can be found in a valley or on a mountaintop, and every place in between.

One of my favorite verses is Psalm 37:4. It reveals that the Lord speaks as powerfully through pleasure as He does through pain. I am learning to not make the mistake of only listening for God's voice when disaster hits, or finally reaching out for His hand when there is no place else to turn. Instead I am realizing more than ever that God's still small voice is in the midst of my daily duties and I have learned to sense His holy presence in places I routinely visit. I have learned to not only be open to God's surprises but also ready and eager to embrace them. When King David said, "Delight yourself in the Lord," the object of David's delight was not a thing: it was the Lord. Learning to delight in the Lord is the completion of the first step toward walking in those holy moments.

Did you know that the bible uses the word "delight" more than 60 times in reference to the Lord? Most of the instances are associated with obeying God's laws, following His commands, rejoicing in His testimonies. I want to walk in that obedience. I also have realized more than ever that another thing God delights in is prayer. (Prov. 15:8) God has answered some big prayers of mine this year. And I am realizing that those answered prayers are holy moments I often fail to recognize. Has God answered any of your prayers? Then you have already experienced a holy moment of your own as well! As you make prayer a part of your life, don't forget to be on the lookout for God's extraordinary response.

It's easy to find evidence of God in the midst of extraordinary circumstances. It's not so easy to detect Him during the ordinary events in our lives. And isn't that where we are most of the time... in the daily ordinary routine of life? We live in the "normal" daily routine where God's voice many times echos somewhere off in the distance, not thundering from the mountain peaks. That is exactly the reason we need to be sensitive to His quiet voice and gentle leading, to those holy moments we often overlook as we rush madly through our daily routines. God longs to intersect our paths with His heavenly interruptions.

I hope as you go through your normal routine today, that you find many holy moments, and many heavenly interruptions. Look for them! They can show up in the most surprising ways. Enjoy those interruptions! God's hand prints are all over them, and He delights in sending them your way. He's already there waiting for you!

Isaiah 65:24 "I will answer them before they even call to me. While they are still talking about their needs, I will answer their prayers!"

Wednesday, June 15, 2011

Wrestling with Worry …. God Wins!

"Mom, they took everything! They took all my computers, cameras, guitars, books....everything." I remember the sound of silence and me gasping for a breath when he gave me the news. Jordan was about to go back to school in Nashville after his spring break. That is until he got the news from his roommate that they had been robbed. They took everything, even the vacuum cleaner. OK, this was not in my plan. I began to take on the worry of it all, and try and figure it all out on my own. My son had the right idea. He went upstairs and he prayed. I should be doing that! As I walked around the room, (pacing is more like it) just asking God what to do, I heard Him say as He always does in that still small voice, "Lisa, don't worry." Don't worry? Me? Oh I wasn't worrying! I was trying to figure out a plan! Really? Nope, I was smack dab in worry world. My husband and I prayed together, and I was determined I would walk in peace through this journey. I had walked through big things this year, hurdled some pretty big hurdles... but what made this journey different is that it touched my child! I think as a Mom we can all agree, when it touches your child, it puts it on a whole new playing field you know? And boy was my trust in God put to the test! "Lisa, don't worry."

You know what I learned through this journey? That peace is faith resting. Faith in a God who does not make mistakes, and who has this whole world in His hands, including my worried world. It releases me to laugh in the darkness, and dance in rain. It makes a way when there doesn't seem to be one. Peace is faith resting in the fact that God will carry this worry for me. Faith counts on it. It is my soul saying "Jesus I will trust you and I will not be afraid" (Isaiah 22:2) Though the mountains fall down and my world disintegrates, I won't fall down and disintegrate, for I am banking on a God who is my refuge and strength, my Rock and my Redeemer. (Psalms 46:1,2; 19:14)

Resting is hard for me. Anyone who knows me knows this. I want to be up and doing something all the time. But through many events this year, including my surgeries and health issues, God has taught me to rest. Not just physically but spiritually. It's a mindset, and I had to learn how to walk in that mindset of rest. Walking in rest, wow! God's work is to provide His serenity in the midst of the storm, my work is to stop trying to manufacture it myself and to be at peace... to rest!

I learned that prayer was the beginning of rest. Have you ever asked the question...."But how can I pray when I am worried?" I have! Prayer is simply verbalizing your worries to God. I have learned this year that instead of worrying... pray. Prayer combats worry by building trust. What I see in my life is that sometimes prayer changes things, but most times, prayer changes me. Many times God does not answer the prayers like I would like. He has a different plan, a much better plan. I have learned that prayer is much more than specific requests I make of the Lord, it's just being with God, enjoying Him, and absorbing His will for me. It's not just something I do, it's somewhere I go to experience the presence of God. I have learned about that lesson this year more than ever. It's always in that presence that my perspectives change and rest becomes so much easier in His arms. I stop the struggle, and I rest. It is at that point I can put even the hardest things for me to release, like my children, in His arms... knowing He will cover them far better than I ever could. It is my job to release them into those loving arms. He will not let me down.

Phil 4:6 talks about praying about our worries with thanksgiving; "In every situation by prayer and petition, with thanksgiving, present your requests to God" Now what does He mean by that? Thank God for worries? No. Thank God for who He is in the midst of the worries. Thank God for His strong eternal shoulders that are perfectly capable of carrying all the burdens of worry in the world.... mine and yours included!

It's been 3 months since we got that bad news about Jordan's apartment. And it has been 3 months of daily miracles. The enemy tried to steal, God restored. There were times we didn't understand why, but we are seeing things more clearly. I know that as we look back years from now, we will see the whole picture even more clearly. God is bigger! I have learned so much through this journey with Jordan. I have learned to trust God with my children in a deeper way. It's such a wonderful thing knowing that God not only carries us, but has our back! Though the enemy comes in like a flood.....God's boat is bigger! It may be tempting to take a swim out there in the sea of worry, but I think I'll stay in the boat, and enjoy the ride. Amazing what you will find in that boat! It's a wonderful worry free ride! Let's go!

Saturday, June 18, 2011

The Day Two Fathers Came to my Rescue

I will never forget the day, I was in the floor sobbing. I was a teenager and just feeling completely overwhelmed. Overwhelmed was an understatement. My self esteem was at an all time low, and I was angry. In all my anger and hurt, sitting there in the floor having a melt down... the door opened and there he was, my precious Dad. He sat in the floor with me, scooped me up in his arms, and cried with me. He cried and he prayed. He didn't know what to say in my fit of rage, so he just loved me and sat there with me asking Jesus to wrap His arms around me too. I remember he sat there for hours praying for me, and I will never forget how his lips quivered as He tried to stop the tears and hold back the hurt from his face so I couldn't see just how deeply he was hurting, because I was hurting.

That day was a turning point for me. I had two Father's running to my rescue that day, and my earthly Father was there to exemplify my Heavenly Father's love. My Dad's arms were the extension of my Heavenly Father's arms. Jesus knew I needed those arms so deeply on that day, and my earthly Father was there to cover.

From the day I was born, my Father has loved me with a love I really cannot describe. The older I get the more I realize how rare a Father's love like his truly is. I have had many people ask me what it was that catapulted me into such a close relationship to Jesus. In fact I was asked this question a few days ago. I can quickly answer that question without hesitation whatsoever. It was because I had an earthly Father who adored Jesus, adored His family, and loved me so deeply, it made it so easy to see how much my heavenly Father could love me. The role my Father has played in my life goes so much further than just being a "Dad". His example to me drew me to Jesus. His love and prayers throughout my life are the reason I know I adore my heavenly Father.

My Dad has been through the darkest of times with me. He never, and I mean never wavered in his love and support. When most Dad's would have fled from the scene, He only loved deeper, and trusted God more. He is one of the most humble men I have ever met. Integrity defines every part of who he is. When I was left to face life alone as a single Mom years ago with a newborn baby and a 2 year old, my father stepped in and prayed and loved my kids and took on the role to guide them. To this day, my kids have the most precious relationship with Jesus and I know my Dad was key in that path of their lives. The same love and guidance I received... they received as well. They to this day remember so vividly memorics of doing things together and how Dad would talk with them about the Lord. I remember seeing Dad hold my kids just like he held me when I was young. I am forever in awe of his love.

One of the most important gifts my dad has given me is his adoration for my mother. He utterly adores the ground she walks on. He has never spoken a cross word to her, and in all my life they have never argued. His affection for her to this day blesses me more than words can convey. I remember his hugs and love pats and sweet words of affection to her growing up. I remember the security I felt knowing they would always be together. Their love for each other really is undefinable. It's so deep. Seeing this love for her helped me not give up when my dreams of marriage were shattered. He taught me to hang on! God had a beautiful plan for my life. God would not leave me and these kids alone and forsake the dream He had placed in my heart. And through his prayers and encouragement... I indeed met and married the man of my dreams. Almost 10 years now I can not believe I could love a man so deeply. He adores my children and together with our beautifully blended family... I once again, know I could not have reached this place without my father.

Dad, if you are reading this I cannot thank you enough. Because of you I didn't give up. That day you held me in your arms when I wanted to give up... changed me in ways you never knew about. You have always thought I was beautiful, even when I didn't. You have always believed in me, even when I didn't. You have walked a very painful journey with me through Mom's cancer the past 2 years, and we grew even closer. The harder life hits you, the closer you get to Jesus. Thank you. Thank you for giving me the most precious gift you could ever have given me. You gave me Jesus.

I have a Godly heritage, I have a wonderful legacy, I have Godly favor on my life because of the life you have led with Mom. The Godly choices you made, and the example you set have laid a path for me and my family that I am forever grateful for.

No matter how old I get I will always love hearing "Hellooo, Sweeeeets!" when I walk through the door! Oh, and the hilarious animal sounds you make every time you see any type of animal. If it's a moo or a bark or meow....or even a quack...it's just such a great memory! (and you don't even know you do it!) I bet you are doing it now reading this!

I love you Dad... thank you for making my life wonderful! Someone said to me the other day...You are so much like your Dad, Lisa. That was the hugest compliment I have ever received. Thank you.

Happy Father's Day Dad... I could not be more proud of who you are and to be your daughter!

Saturday, July 2, 2011

China, Emergency Surgery... and Jesus

 As I stood there pouring my cup of coffee and going over the long list of things I had do get done that day, I heard that still small voice, not so still and quiet saying... "Go now Lisa, Go NOW! Go check on Kerrigan!" Kerrigan had been through what was supposed to be a routine tonsillectomy but it turned out to not be the case. After a week of struggling she finally was resting... I thought. I had only on a few occasions felt the prompting in my spirit to this degree. I dropped my coffee, literally, and ran. I found her on the couch in a pool of blood. It was coming out of her nose, out of her mouth... it looked like a crime scene. I remember at that very moment just saying out loud "Oh Jesus, help me... help me." It was all I could get out. In a few hours after that moment she had been rushed through surgery and was in recovery. An artery had not been cauterized properly and opened up... the bleeding was horrendous. Seeing her frail body lying there so pale, was something I will never forget.

On this same day, I was to see my oldest daughter off for the rest of the summer, to Beijing, China. We had planned a time that afternoon to say our goodbyes and spend some time together. I literally in a 15 minute span of time was saying goodbye to my oldest as she left for her trip, and another goodbye to my youngest as she was wheeled into emergency surgery.

I can only tell you that this journey today took me once again to a place with Jesus that no words can describe. It was a deeper place of trust and rest. I remember many years ago, in a bible study, being told that during times like these I should stay strong, start quoting scripture, and have faith. I memorized mountains of scriptures, which I am so thankful I did, and was prepared. But as I stood there today seeing my daughter helpless, all I could say was "Oh Jesus... help me". I couldn't remember one of those scriptures. Just "Jesus!" And you know what? That was all I needed. I cannot begin to tell you the presence that filled that room as I cried out His name for help. He knew what was in my heart, He knew how desperately I needed Him. I truly believe the most elaborate of prayers is just the name of Jesus. I didn't have to quote a long passage of scripture, I didn't have to start praying a big worded prayer to be heard... all I needed was Jesus.

Was I strong? It depends on what you define as strong. I stayed strong throughout the whole ordeal, and then I let myself fall apart. I have a place in my closet that I reserve for "ugly cries". You know, those cries where your soul just lets go and it comes from your belly? (Groanings too deep for words: Romans 8:26) Yep, one of those cries. Jesus always meets me there, and I never feel guilty for letting go. I have felt so close to Him in that prayer closet at times it is like I can feel His breath on my face.

I have had to release my children to God in a way like never before. From China to Emergency surgery... they are in His hands. It's easy to say, hard to do. But as soon as I completely release them... there is a peace like never before. What greater hands could I place them in?

Kerrigan is resting peacefully, Laura made it to Beijing. I made it through another journey with Jesus realizing more than ever that there is such a freedom and peace in walking this journey with Him. There is no bondage in this walk, only freedom and miracles waiting. If I forget to quote some scriptures during a crisis, or if I fall apart and cry in His arms... He is there regardless. I have never felt His presence more strongly than when I just cry out His name. Oh the precious name of Jesus. No matter what journey awaits me today, tomorrow or the next. He will be enough....

I can still hear my sweet Grandma's voice singing as she sewed in her chair...

Jesus Jesus Jesus, there's just
something about that name.
Master, Saviour, Jesus, like the
fragrance after the rain
Jesus, Jesus, Jesus, let all heaven and
earth proclaim
Kings and kingdoms will pass away
But there's something about that Name!

Saturday, July 30, 2011

Choose Happy!

I gave her a big kiss as she was taken back for yet another test. Before she went in, we had the conversation that no matter what happened, what the results, she would be fine. She chose to remain in that "happy place" with Jesus, and not miss a second of what He had in store for her. My Mom lives in that "happy place" every day of her life.

As I sat in the waiting room, I began to think about my Mom, and the things she instilled in me. I began to thank God that I always saw her choose that place of happiness, no matter what. My Mom has been through so many trials these past 2 years in her battle with cancer, and if ever there was a time to go to the "pity party" place, it could have been these years. But she refused. And the result? Joy, peace, blessing, trust, grace, ministry, miracles... and the list goes on.

I don't think it was by accident that a precious 84 year old man came over to me in the waiting room and sat beside me. He was tall, and thin, and very frail. His hands trembled as he shook my hand and introduced himself. His name was Bob. Bob was one of the kindest men I have ever met. In the course of the 2 hour wait, we talked. He told me about his life, and my mouth was open in awe of all he had walked through. His full time job now? Taking care of his very ill wife who was in surgery while we were talking. With all the adversity Bob had gone through, he kept saying over and over....

"But you know? Life is a choice, you can be happy... or you can be miserable. I choose happy." He had a sparkle in his eyes, and it was very evident he chose "Happy." He had been married to his wife 60 years, and adored her. The only time he teared up was when he talked of possibly losing her. But then he followed it with "But Miss Lisa, I will choose happy even then. And when I can't humanly choose Happy because of a broken heart... God will choose happy for me." OK, by then... I am going for the Kleenex. Bob became my dear friend during this 2 hour wait. I pray for him everyday and his sweet wife, and am so thankful for our time together. When I left the hospital I passed his room and he was kneeling over the hospital bed where his wife was. He was kissing her hands and stroking the hair out of her face. Yes, he adored her, it was obvious. Bob chose "Happy", and love oozed out of that man to all he encountered.

I am glad he encountered me!

As I drove home that day, my heart was so full. I reflected upon the events of my summer... some good, some not so good. And what I realized is that on those "not so good" times, when I chose "happy", God gave me such strength, such favor, and such grace. It was like a gift He poured down for me. I felt His favor on me as I chose to go the high road, and delight in Him in the hardest of circumstances. It's a simple thing to say and yet at times very difficult to do. But the reward is amazing! Life changes, things change, the future changes, God opens doors, and it's astounding what happens!

No wonder the enemy tries to divert us with trivial things that trip us up from day to day! He wants us to miss this amazing gift God has waiting for us! He knows how powerful "happy" is and he wants us to miss it all!

Through Mom's cancer, to my own health struggles... perspectives change, priorities change. I have learned to savor every single second of life like never before and not waste a minute. There is no time to stay in a cloud of negativity. I want to run from it. I know what it does. It feeds like a cancer, and blocks what God wants to do in our lives. When I see friends or family there, my heart breaks because I know what they are missing. LIFE! HAPPINESS! MIRACLES! JESUS! Yes, even through the darkest of times... there is a happy place. It was that happy place that saved my life when it was so dark I couldn't see light.

I encourage you to find those arms of Jesus and snuggle in to that happy place that only He can give. No matter what you are going through... that happy place leads to freedom and miracles you never dreamed possible. And when you can't do it on your own... He can do it for you. He's good at that.

One of my favorite quotes is "When you change the way you look at things, the things you look at change". God, may we all see things through your eyes, and love with your heart. You delight in a life of cartwheels and laughter... in fact I feel a cartwheel comin' on now. See you in "the happy place!"

And for those wondering about Mom's test results... benign! Tests came back great! Isn't God good!!!

Saturday, August 6, 2011

The Hug That Started a Life Changing Journey...

I remember the day so vividly. It was a few months ago, and I was leaving the doctor's office. It wasn't a fun visit, and quite frankly I was a bit low from all the tests that were being run. I got into the elevator and pushed the button for the lobby. Then I heard a faint whisper as we began to lower to the floors below. "Mommy, I think that lady needs a hug." I looked down and a precious little girl with big blue eyes was looking at me. She was probably in kindergarten. Her mother quickly said "Shhh, don't bother the lady" in a stern voice. By the 3rd floor the little girl was pulling on her mother's skirt... "Please Mommy, can I give the lady a hug?" And before her Mother answered, I said to her "Ya know, I'd love a hug!" A smile crept on the Mother's face. I knelt down to hug this precious little girl and she grabbed my neck so hard I could hardly breathe! She gave bear hugs a new meaning. This little girl knew.... she knew I needed this hug today, and by golly there was nothing that was going to stop her! Boldness! Oh for that childlike boldness and faith! God delights in that!

Well, not only did this little girl make my day that day, she made me realize even more the impact that just a hug, or a smile can make on somebody's day. I became more sensitive that day to look around at others. Doesn't it seem that so many people go throughout their day with no joy? People work hard, feel unappreciated, and sometimes wonder if they even have a purpose. So I did a little project this summer. Some call it "pay it forward" some call it "random acts of kindness", others may call it planting seeds. All I know is that I wanted to let others know they mattered... just like that little girl in the elevator made me feel that day I was feeling low. I wanted to get out of my comfort zone and I prayed God would show me those needing a "random act of kindness." I learned that He answers those prayers very quickly. God swung the doors wide open! And little did I know the healing that would come from it all would be mine.

It started with helping my elderly neighbor with her trash during the week. It grew to going to nursing homes... random nursing homes. I just went down the halls and gave hugs. I brought Holly with me and they adored her! The precious residents did the rest. I love to listen to life stories. What made these people who they are today? Boy did I hear wonderful stories! One dear man kept saying "Thank you for listening to me... nobody ever listens to me anymore." His eyes brightened and he sparkled. I think he felt just like I felt the day I got that wonderful hug from the little girl. He mattered! And I was blessed beyond words by his story. I looked behind me as Holly and I left and about 7 residents were waving goodbye, saying "Please come back!" Oh I will come back, that's for sure.

One day as I was driving in this 107 degree heat. I saw construction workers in this horrible heat working feverishly. I whispered out loud... "Thank you Lord, for the people who do this!" And I got the response... "Lisa, why don't you thank them yourself?" What? Wow. How Lord? Funny, I was parked right in front of a grocery store so I jumped out of my car, ran in and got cold waters and Gatorade, and loaded up. I stopped at places throughout the day and handed out those waters and Gatorades. The looks on the faces of these people will be etched in my mind forever. All I said was "Thank you! What you do matters!" and off I went. I don't know if those waters did for those people what they did for me even, but I just felt God's presence in amazing ways through this journey. It was as if He was just guiding, directing, placing, and blessing each and every event in my day.... and indeed He was. This project was not just for others... He was doing a work in my heart as well. There was healing going on! Go figure :)

My daughter and I were in the store one day getting a desk for her room. The man helping us get the big box down was NOT happy. In fact my daughter said "Mom, I don't think we better bother him, he's not happy." But not only did we need help with our desk, but why not let this man know he was appreciated for the help he would give? So I went over and he looked at me with a huge grimace. My daughter was right, he was NOT happy. He said "What do you want?" I asked if he could help us load up the box. He grumbled like Mr. Scrooge under his breath and got the cart. As he was rolling it down the isle for us I said... "Sir, thank you for what you do.... and thank you for helping us. I appreciate you." And he replied "You are the first person in months to thank to me Ma'am". And then he started talking... he talked about the lady who had just come in and screamed at him because they didn't have the lamp she wanted... and before we knew it we were up at the front, laughing with all the other checkers around. Turns out this guy had a hilarious sense of humor!! He wasn't a scrooge after all! He walked the desk out to our car and loaded it up for us. Then he shook my hand and said "Miss, thank you for helping me remember I can laugh... and I really am a pretty funny guy!" I said, "Yes you are! And a very appreciated one at that!" I tried to look cool as I walked over to get into the car, because my lip was twitching all over the place and I knew the tears would follow. It was so touching to my heart, I could hardly hold it in. All he needed was a simple kind word. That's all it took!

Was this journey easy everyday? No. The enemy loves to put things even negative people in our lives to trip us up. Oh he loves the art of distraction. There were days I woke up in so much physical pain from my journey with arthritis and celiacs that I thought, I won't be able to do this today. I can't even get out of bed! And you know what I found? I took the first step, and usually it was on those days the most miracles happened! And by the end of the day I was in no pain. I tell you folks... giving heals! Encouraging heals! Getting out of one's selfish comfort zone... heals! Staying in that happy place... heals! Jesus... heals! And boy does He give the grace to walk it all out on those hard hard days.

What lessons I have learned this summer! The most life changing gifts one can give are free, they touch the recipient's heart but they end up changing the giver's heart as well, and they last a lifetime... their echos are heard and felt for eternity. I have met more friends on this journey, and have never been more amazed at how many wonderful people are out there!

I recommend this to anyone and everyone. Give it a try! I wake up each morning excited for what people God will place in my life each day. What journeys He will take me on. My family is on this journey with me as well now... and I love hearing the stories at the end of each day. And I chuckle to myself as I write this because yesterday, I made a run for Starbucks. I realized I left my purse at home and was going through my change in the car. As I got up to the window, looking frantically for the money, I saw a big smile looking at me. "Ma'am, your coffee has been paid for, by the man ahead of you." Are there words for that? If there are I can't find them. Except.... that's just the way God does it. I serve an amazing God! Even if you expect nothing in return... the blessing you will receive will amaze you. Get ready!

I hope I see that little girl again someday... I am going to give her the best hug ever. She has no idea what that hug started, and what the hug will continue for the rest of my life. See you on the journey... and when I do, I will give you a great big hug!

Sunday, September 11, 2011

Can I Do This Lord? The Journey I Faced as a Single Mom...

I remember the day like it was yesterday.... that drive from Texas to Tulsa almost 20 years ago...with 2 babies. My son just a few months old, and my daughter just 22 months old. It was just the three of us now. In her sweet little voice, my daughter whispered to me "Mommy, are we going bye bye?" My heart broke. As my parents drove the van, I sat in the back seat and hung onto my babies for dear life. My world had literally stopped. How could I raise them alone? They were babies! How could we have been left? Why? How could he leave us? My husband had chosen an affair over his family and now, I had to pick up the pieces... I had no choice. Of course my self esteem was shattered with all the feelings one has when an affair occurs. But I can only say that it was at that moment, when I passed the Oklahoma state line, that my world changed, forever. I heard the still small voice of the Holy Spirit whisper to my heart.... "I will carry you now Lisa. I will take you to new places with your children that you never dreamed possible, and I will open doors... I will heal and I will guide and teach you things that will change your life forever....don't let go of your dream." Don't let go of my dream? What? But Lord, my dream was shattered? He saw much further than I did, and He knew the dream He had placed in my heart all along. He wanted to bring it to pass. It was my job to let Him. It was my job to give Him the brushes and let Him paint the new picture on this blank canvas before me... with my babies. Little did I know it would be more than just a picture, it would be a masterpiece.

I remember those days like they were yesterday. Working two jobs, getting those babies up everyday and getting them to school. I remember being so tired that my toenails even hurt, and knowing I had to get the kids home, get homework done, get dinner on the table, and spend quality time with them. I remember the pressure of making it financially on my own. I remember the loneliness when the kids were all in bed and it was just me.

You know what is amazing though? When I look back on those years of single parenting now, and I see the picture God was painting all along, I stand in amazement. It was at that very moment of being left and alone and clutching onto Jesus with every fiber of my being that taught me the greatest lessons that I still lean on to this day. And what exactly can one learn from being left with 2 small babies to raise?

I learned that 2 Corinthians 12:9 is true. He pours out His grace in proportion to what we need. And I needed a truck load of grace. He cared so deeply for me and saw my extreme need for Him as His opportunity to provide. And He had more than enough grace to walk me through this journey. We were tucked safely under His wings. And He was not letting go.

I learned how to forgive. Oh this was a biggie for me. My children could pick up on the angry feelings I had and carried. I will go so far as to say I not only walked through anger, I walked through rage. I was mad! When I wanted to speak badly of their father, I knew I couldn't. He was still their father. God literally took my hand on this one and step by step peeled away the layers of unforgiveness until I walked in freedom. I could not have done it without the Holy Spirit guiding me every step of the way. There is freedom in forgiveness. I knew the second that weight was lifted off of my shoulders, I had forgiven. I could breathe! I realized that forgiveness can be a daily journey though. When tempted to take that anger back on, God was there to take it for me... daily. There were some days on that journey I literally had to say, Jesus, right now I can't do this, can you? And He would take it from there. The Holy Spirit became real to me in ways that forever changed my life. When in my own strength I couldn't, He could. 2 Corinthians 12:10

I learned how important getting involved in a great home church really is. Not only was it a place for healing for me but I realized that I could be used by God even in my broken state! We were in church when the doors opened, and we were involved. I developed friendships that were healthy and life long. My children were involved and loving it! Singing on the praise and worship team was instrumental in so much of my healing. We were surrounded with love and support, and this was literally a life line for us. God used that church to help us in more ways that I can even express.

I learned that there is laughter and joy, even in the hard times. One day, feeling overwhelmed, I started to cry. I cried one of those "ugly" cries where you can hardly breathe. I got a glimpse of myself in the mirror and how my face was all shriveled up like a prune, and how ridiculous I looked. It cracked me up! I went from uncontrollable tears to uncontrollable laughter! My kids came in and we just laughed! In fact I could not even remember why I was crying in the first place. It was at that moment that I realized that I could laugh! It was healing! And I could teach my children how to laugh! I remember funny dances we would make up together, silly songs we would sing, bible verses we would memorize with hand motions, cookies we would bake with silly faces... and laughter filled the house. And you know what my kids remember to this day most? The laughter and the love in our home. And when we talk about that love and laughter during that season, it gets me every time. They remember it with detail.

Laughter is healing. And I learned that even when my heart was breaking, I could laugh, and the joy of the Lord really would be my strength. Many have asked me how I find laughter in tough journeys. I found it during this season of my life. It was what got me through. This kind of laughter comes from the soul, where Jesus has a grip. There really is no adjective to describe it. It carried us through the journey then, and it carries us through our journey now.

I think the biggest thing I learned through this journey was to not let go of my dream. Even though it seemed the dream was crushed, it was not. God was just going to find a different way to bring that dream into fruition. Trust me, He will blow your mind. Just don't let go! Don't listen to the lies of the enemy that you will never see that dream come to pass. As I gave the Lord those brushes to paint my masterpiece, He did! And what a masterpiece He painted! I have 4 children and a daughter in law now who are all passionate for Jesus, a husband who was sent from heaven, and 3 dogs who, yes, are also part of that beautiful picture! I look at that dream everyday in awe and wonder and thankfulness. I also remember those things I learned in the 10 years I walked through the journey of single parenting. I could not have made that journey without Jesus.

To all my dear friends walking through the journey of single parenting, I want to encourage you! There is hope! There is laughter! There is strength! There are miracles! There is a dream to be fulfilled! There is a masterpiece in the making! Just let go of the brushes and watch Him paint! I promise you, you will be amazed! Van Gogh and Da Vinci have nothing on what God is painting for you and your children.

Friday, September 30, 2011

Today God Sent a Miracle My Way... Her Name Was Emily.

I was so honored to be asked to help with a special needs gym class today with Holly (my service dog in training). These children are not disabled, that word just doesn't describe these children. They are some of the most abled children I have ever met. There was one little girl named Emily who wanted to run around the track so badly with all the others, but went very slow because of her crutches and could never make it around. We found a way! Holly walked beside her and the little girl leaned on Holly the entire way for extra support. At times Emily would stop and just wrap her arms around Holly and kiss her on the head. Holly was in heaven, and the connection between these two had me wiping tears. Holly worked like she has never worked before. It was like she was one with this precious child. The smile on Emily's face was as big as the smile on Holly's face. It was the first time Emily ever made it around that track! When we finished, the little girl grabbed my hand and said "Mrs. Lisa, do you know that Holly loves Jesus?" Choked up I got out a "Why yes she does!" Then she said, "Mrs. Lisa, you love Jesus too! Do you know how I know?" I replied... "How?" And those big blue eyes looked up at me and said, "Because I see your hearts, and there's sunshine in there... that's where Jesus lives... isn't that neat? Mrs. Lisa, I love Jesus too! He makes me happy everyday!" OK, so by now I am in one of those ugly cries... you know where you are gasping for air? I hugged that sweet little girl with everything I had, and Holly did too! She had no idea how deeply she had just blessed my heart. After a morning with these precious children... I honestly don't think my heart could be any more full. And I honestly love Jesus with a more wild abandon love than ever because of what Emily taught me. How could one be around a child like Emily and not want to love Jesus more? I asked her teacher if she was always this happy. And her reply was "She's the light of the classroom". Her disability hinders her the most physically, but her spirit makes up for it all. I have never seen anyone more alive and happy and abled in my life. I have thought about Emily all day.

It is days like these that remind me of how much I want to run from negativity, drama and strife. I want to focus on what really matters and never waste a second of this life. It is but a vapor, so very short. As Emily said I want to live in the sunshine where Jesus lives, and I want to make the moments matter. On the way home I looked over at Holly, and she looked at me with that angelic grin that only Holly can give, and I knew she was feeling that same joy I was. It was definitely a day full of sunshine! We were both basking in it together......

Wednesday, November 16, 2011

A Christmas Lesson Learned… in the Checkout Line

"You are getting those? Are you kidding me? How can you do that? It's way too early!" Yes, those were the words I received, with a look of disdain to go with it, as I was standing in line to check out. I felt like I should be wearing a helmet in case objects were thrown at me. And what exactly did I have that was setting this dear lady into a rage? I had tinsel and ribbon for the Christmas tree. I not only had a lady who was mad at my purchase, but a line of 8 people ahead of me! This was going to be a very long wait. Would I live through it? Would I have any missing body parts after I got checked out?

I was a bit thrown back on this one, but now, I understand why I had a very long wait ahead of me. God knew exactly what He was doing. As I stood there, I looked around at the packed store and I saw sad faces everywhere. I saw people mad and angry at the crowd and the long wait. I even saw a couple in the next line over arguing about the fact that Christmas trees were up and it was a tragedy to start the holidays so early. I thought, "Wow, if they see what's in my cart, I will not make it out of here alive!" It made my heart sink. Should I run, hide, duck for cover?

I am one of those people, yes I will admit, that decorates my Christmas tree November 1st! Some years it's decorated on Halloween! I can hear things being thrown at me now. I LOVE the holidays! I love putting that tree up every year. I am the one belting out Michael Bublé Christmas tunes the first of November. And the one who has tinsel in my cart at the store while everyone else is buying their Halloween candy. Many have asked "What is wrong with you, Lisa?!" Good question!

As I was standing in line, the Lord took me down Memory Lane! I began the journey in my mind of all the Christmas seasons in my life. The seasons were filled with many memories! There were some years we faced many trials. Some years there was loss. There were the years I faced it as a single Mom, not by choice, and wondered how we would even have a Christmas. The years of my Mom's fight with cancer, and my battle with my own health issues. But even through those trials, what a joy the Christmas season was! I began thinking about it all. What made those difficult Christmas seasons happy?

Growing up, no matter what, my Mom and Dad made it about Jesus. No matter what the circumstance, it was about family, giving, and love. I will never forget the Christmas they announced that we would be giving our Christmas to a family that could not have a Christmas of their own. I remember my reaction. "ARE YOU KIDDING ME?" I know, I wish I could say I danced around with glee at this news. I will say this though, when I saw that single Mother and those 4 children open their gifts that Christmas, and eat the meal we prepared, and help us decorate the tree we put up for them... my life changed. My Christmas was redefined. I don't think my Mom and Dad know how deeply that Christmas impacted my life. I was only in Jr. High during that Christmas, but it was then that it all made sense to me. This is what the Christmas season was all about. This was what it should be like all year long.

As I was driving home one day, my daughter and I began talking about the Christmas season. She was working on math, and she looked over at me and said "Mom, I think people need to learn about Christmas banking. I think that if they realized it was not about purchasing but investing, they would not think it had become so about money and purchasing gifts." By George, I think she's got it! We came to the conclusion that Christmas is only as materialized as we make it. I actually had tears rolling down my face by the time we had reached the house. It was about investing. Investing in the lives of others, investing in things that matter and are eternal. Those gifts may not fill the room with wrapping paper and boxes, they fill it with things that last an eternity, and are investments into the kingdom of heaven!

My husband and I made an announcement to the kids a few weeks ago that we decided to have a Christmas without purchases. It would be about investing this year, like the Christmas that changed my life when I was young. I thought I would get the same reaction I gave my parents years ago... "ARE YOU KIDDING?" And quite frankly braced myself for their reaction. Boy was I surprised. I remember hearing, "Hey, let's make new traditions! Let's make a Christmas brunch together!... Let's make our gifts this year!"... and the ideas were flowing. (and I was running for the Kleenex!) Seeing the smiles, hearing the laughter that day on the 1st week of November, with the tree up and lighted... my Christmas had been made, two months early.

I made it to the front of the line, and by this time had a smile on my face. For in that 20 minutes of waiting, I realized even more how thankful I was to be celebrating the one who invested His life for me. I left that store with not only tinsel for the Christmas tree but with a new perspective, and a new excitement for this season. And yes, I belted my Michael Bublé tunes all the way to the car. And I even saw a little smile come over the face of the lady who was angry at me in line as I was leaving. Amazing what God can teach us, even in the checkout line at a store. He invests so much into my life everyday, now it's my turn.

Friday, November 25, 2011

Overwhelmed or Overshadowed... You Decide

He shall cover you with His feathers...

and under His wings you shall find refuge.

Psalm 91:4

As I was running very early this morning, what was usually a very quiet run, was filled with the sound of cars, and traffic. It was 6:30 am! Then the two words hit me. "Black Friday!" Wow. One neighbor was running frantically out of her house, yelling... "Hurry up, we are late!" Her coffee was spilling everywhere as she tried to open the car door. Her teenage son looked at her and said "Mom, this is so not fun." His arms were folded and he was not about to have a good day. I waved as I went by and she said to me "Oh how I hate the holidays!"

I began thinking to myself about the holiday season. To many this holiday is a difficult one. What may be Christmas carols and Christmas baking to one person, may mean sitting at a hospital for another, or dealing with the death of a loved one, a marriage, or even feeling like a dream has died. To some it may bring great memories, to others... memories that bring raw feelings to the surface that are easily buried during the year, yet rise to the surface during the holiday season.

Then I began to think about my own stresses, and how God was dealing with me. If there is one thing God is showing me how to do more when I am completely overwhelmed, when every task is too daunting, and problems seem insurmountable... it is to go to the deep place with Him. I don't have to shout out "Lord, I am having a pity party now... a little help please?" He's already at the party and knows exactly what I am doing. It is in that place that I hear Him remind me "Lisa when you are overwhelmed, remember... you are overshadowed!" I am under His wings! And as I rest in His presence, under those mighty wings, that peace that passes all understanding wraps around me like a warm blanket and fills me with the hope that I can make it through anything! Anything! And believe me, there have been many "anythings" this year. Those wings have been there as my comforter. And there were days I needed Him to be my helper, my healer, and my friend. He's been them all.

My prayer for my friends and family this holiday season is that when that overwhelming feeling presses in.... remember that you are overshadowed! When we put on the garment of praise under His wings, heaviness disappears. In fact it is easy to forget what we were overwhelmed about in the first place when we are under those wings in an attitude of praise. I have seen it work this year in ways I can't even describe. Through health situations I thought I could not even face... He overshadowed me. Through journeys I faced with questions... He overshadowed me. He will do the same for you. Enjoy this holiday season knowing you are in a very safe place where His arms won't let go. What a wonderful place to be, under the shadow of the almighty. Makes it easy to focus on the one who gave us life. That's what it's all about anyway.

Thursday, December 1, 2011

Yes Lord, I'll Serve You... Even in a Chicken Suit!

She looked up at me with sparkling eyes and said "I love you chicken lady! And I sure love your dog!" She then leaned over and kissed my cheek, and Holly even got a kiss too! My heart was full and in a million years I never dreamed I'd be here... in a chicken suit with my dog singing songs with a group of senior citizens. But I was not surprised... only amazed at how God answers prayer.

I cannot begin to tell you the countless stories of God's provision in my life this year. But I honestly think the most profound of that provision came when I wanted to help others, and needed a financial miracle to help it happen. I have learned to never underestimate God's answers. And never be surprised... His provision can come in the most unexpected ways. (Even in comical ways... go figure!)

My precious friend and I had coffee one day and the tears were flowing. She was hurting and my heart was breaking with her. She had lost her job and was overwhelmed. We prayed together and as I hugged her tight... under my breath I was saying to God, "Oh Lord, I wish I had some money to help her. I wish I could do something!" I didn't feel a bolt of thunder roll or a mighty wind swoosh through with a miracle, but I can tell you... God heard our hearts cry that day, and He began to answer both of our prayers. I remember driving home with a heart of continued prayer for my friend, and I heard the Lord just whisper to my heart, "Are you willing Lisa?" Willing Lord? I am always willing to serve and help you Lord! Little did I know what He had in store... to answer my prayer... to help my friend.

It all began with my chicken suit. That chicken suit I have in my closet that I love to wear in the winter because it is so warm and cozy. Do I look ridiculous? Yes. But I love my warm chicken suit. It somehow makes me smile on those "hard to smile" days. So why was I surprised a chicken suit would be involved in God's answer to my prayer?

The phone rang one day and it was one of my friends who was laughing at a picture she saw of me on Facebook wearing my chicken suit. She said to me "There is no way you would ever wear that thing out is there?" Are you kidding? Of course I would! She is involved in children's ministry and is a precious friend. She said to me "Lisa, I will give you $100.00 if you wear that suit to Starbucks and have coffee!" "I said to her... "You know I will do this, why are you going to pay me?" And her reply was "Lisa, sometimes God works in mysterious ways." I started to challenge her and was immediately stopped as the Lord reminded me of the prayer I prayed... "I wish I had money to bless my friend..." This was His answer for me to help! I could give that $100.00 to my friend to help her!

Well you can finish the rest of the story I am sure. That one visit to Starbucks in my chicken suit was the open door to provision to help my friends. I had a precious lady ask me if I would ever come to a nursing home or a hospital in my chicken suit with my service dog. She knew I had Holly because she had seen me there before with her. Of course I would! God was opening doors out of the blue, as only He can open! This was amazing and hilarious at the same time! A chicken lady with a service dog... that most definitely is creative, Lord. Well it turns out that this combination brings smiles to many hearts. How can one not laugh at the picture of it all? Isn't God just so creative?

As I sit here today writing this blog, I have tears in my eyes as I think about how He provided the money for me to give to others. I was able to help some dear friends in ways I otherwise could not. I didn't have the resources, but He did! And He knew the reward I would receive was not about the money I was blessed with to help others, but the heart blessing I received because of it. How can you put a price on the smiles I saw, the hugs I received, the laughs I laughed with people, and the prayers I got to pray with those hurting? You can't... no price can be put on that.

I have learned to never put God in a box. He will far surpass the limitations I put on Him. He's bigger, He's more creative, He's always one step ahead of me. Whether you are one in need, or one who wants to help, I challenge you to just ask. Just ask Him for help. Ask Him for the provision you need. He will help you in ways you never dreamed. And I promise you... you will have fun on the journey. More fun than you ever imagined! Take it from the chicken lady with a service dog... it's a journey that will change your life!

Sunday, December 11, 2011

Santa Claus and the Finish Line

I was on mile 3 of the run. I was looking around at the runners beside me thinking to myself, "Boy I love these runs!" Then all at once I felt my left foot begin to go numb. "Oh this is great Lord, please not today, not on this run... not now!" I then knew what would come next... my leg would go. That's when I'd get creative and hop until the feeling came back. I knew what to do, I had done it so many times before. It was the Jingle Bell Run, and everyone was dressed up in Christmas costumes. In fact I was delighted to have Santa, the Grinch, and a snowman running with me. But as my speed slowed and the hopping began, Santa asked me if I needed help. "Oh, it will pass... go on without me." He was an elderly little Santa, (but man could he run!) He didn't want to leave without helping. So I hopped, and he jogged slowly with me until the feeling came back and I was on my way again... just minus the snowman and the Grinch.

We had a great talk, Santa and I. We talked about the seasons of life. He had struggled with health issues this past year just as I had. We also talked about how God had been faithful through it all. He suffered with a disease called ankylosing spondylitis. I'd heard those words before as I sat on the doctors table being diagnosed with that long word over a year ago... one I couldn't even pronounce. That's why he stayed with me on this run. He knew what it was like to hop in races. He'd been there. And he didn't leave my side. He told me he remembered a race that he literally hopped for a mile until the feeling came back. We laughed at the humorous things that we had gone through. It was so fun to laugh about it.

As we parted ways after the run, I was so thankful for the people God had strategically placed in my life to help me along the way. I also began thinking about this season of life that I am in. Yes there have been some hard blows, really hard blows, but as I sat on the curb catching my breath I realized that God was teaching me how to rest... how to trust... how to have faith like never before. This season was not going to be defined by the hard blows, but by the life changing things God was teaching me about trusting... and resting in Him.

Someone once said to me that to rest meant I wasn't trusting... I wasn't moving. I needed to run this race! Hmmm. I agree that running the race is important... but rest is a part of the race sometimes. A very important part. Sometimes the most important part! Just as I was at a point where I physically could not run in the race today... I had to take a break, hop for awhile, even sit by the curb for a minute.. and start back up when my body would let me again. If I hadn't I would have been run over by the other runners.

The enemy would love to run me over in life. I have seen him try on many occasions this year. I realize that sometimes resting takes practice. I am not a good "rester". Those of you who know me, know how true this is. God has had to help me on this one.

I did a study on resting in the presence of God. And I was amazed when I learned that rest can be a weapon! A weapon we use in the battles that the enemy throws in our path to defeat us. It is a sword in our hand. Resting never allows the opposition to dictate how we think or feel. Never. It brings all negativity to a standstill. It has the best jab ever. It has the confidence and the assurance to say. "No, you are not coming in" when the enemy comes knocking.

When we enter into the rest of God, we are at peace within His shadow. The Bible even serves to remind us in 1 Kings 5:4 that God will give rest to us on every side and that there will be no adversary or disaster that will be able to penetrate His great love. He goes before us in every situation to make the crooked paths straight.

So as I sit here thinking about this run today. I have to chuckle. I finished in record time (even with my resting in the middle). And wouldn't you know, I ran through that finish line with Santa Claus. Does it get better than that? God knew I needed some help today... and as He always does... He came through once again. Thank you God for rest. Your arms are big, your peace indescribable, and your healing complete.

My prayer is that whatever season you are facing, no matter how insurmountable the hurdles and race you are in may seem... that you find rest. Your miracle is waiting there. I promise...you will not only win the race victoriously... you will cross the finish line in record time! God won't let you down.

Saturday, December 31, 2011

It is Well ….

As I sat in my prayer chair in the early morning this New Year's Eve, I could hear her sweet voice singing as if she were right next to me. I could hear the stories she would tell me of her life and how Jesus never left her side. My precious Grandmother would always say "Lisa, it is well with my soul... no matter what." And one always knew, it truly was... always well with her soul. Until the day she died, no matter what she faced, her soul walked out peace with her Savior.

Jesus knew I needed to be reminded of this today. My heart was in pity party mode today, not New Year's party mode. I am a planner, and my big plans for Christmas vacation were a bit altered. I found myself down the entire break with pneumonia. Not in the plan. I began to go down the "Why God?" road, until I played the song my sweet Grandma used to sing. "It is well with my soul".

This song is about the testimony of a man who experienced a series of life-altering, tragic events. He lost his first son at the age of only four. Then without much of a moment to catch his breath, he also lost his financial livelihood and ability to properly care for his family. Subsequently then just two years later, as his wife and daughters traveled across the seas, the ship they were on sank and all four of his daughters died. His wife, the only survivor, sent the tragic news ahead to him and that she was the only one to make it home to him.

One would think that this man would have been crushed, quite possibly, for the rest of his life. And no doubt his heart grieved for the loss of his children. But the true testament of this man's character is what his heart posture produced through the process of it all. Take a look at what flowed out from the heart of this man as he then traveled back by ship himself to meet his grieving wife, passing the very area where his daughters had died.

Horatio Spafford penned these words aboard the ship to meet his wife:

When peace, like a river, attendeth my way,
When sorrows like sea billows roll;
Whatever my lot, Thou has taught me to say,
It is well, it is well, with my soul
It is well, with my soul,
It is well, it is well, with my soul.
Though Satan should buffet, though trials should come,
Let this blest assurance control,
That Christ has regarded my helpless estate,
And hath shed His own blood for my soul.
My sin, oh, the bliss of this glorious thought!
My sin, not in part but the whole,

Is nailed to the cross, and I bear it no more,
Praise the Lord, praise the Lord, O my soul!
For me, be it Christ, be it Christ hence to live:
If Jordan above me shall roll,
No pang shall be mine, for in death as in life
Thou wilt whisper Thy peace to my soul.
But, Lord, 'tis for Thee, for Thy coming we wait,
The sky, not the grave, is our goal;
Oh, trump of the angel! Oh, voice of the Lord!
Blessed hope, blessed rest of my soul!
And Lord, haste the day when my faith shall be sight,
The clouds be rolled back as a scroll;
The trump shall resound, and the Lord shall descend,
Even so, it is well with my soul.

As I sat listening to the words of this song this morning, I was touched by the determination this man had in cultivating a lasting and intimate relationship with God. It was evident in how he lived his life and how he responded to even the darkest moments in his life. He did not allow his circumstances to dictate to him how he would behave and who he would become; rather, he found his anchor and true identity resting in His relationship with Jesus.

As this year nears its end and we reflect upon all that it has brought our way, may we rest in the peace of God's embrace and sweetly declare, "It is well with my soul." For whether it is peace like a river or sorrows like sea billows that we have encountered, even still, in relationship to Him, it is well because we know that God is passionately intentional about causing all things to work together for our good. Now that's cause for a celebration! It's going to be a great 2012!

Sunday, January 22, 2012

Keeping it Simple …. in a Life Full of Distractions

Just as I do each morning, I was on my way upstairs to pray for each of my children. I go into their rooms each morning when they are gone and I spend time in prayer for them. Some days I am in there for minutes, some days for hours. But today as I went into my son's room... there it was on his desk. I gasped in surprise! It was beautiful! How did he get this gem? It was a very old typewriter. It was in mint condition and it was just like my grandmother owned. I had typed on a typewriter like this before! I was instantly taken down memory lane. It was heavenly! As I sat there in the quiet, I looked around the room. The computer, T.V., electronic equipment were all around, but center stage was that beautiful old typewriter. I found out later he had purchased it for $25.00 at an estate sale. I could only imagine the stories this old typewriter could tell. It was apparent by the worn ribbon that it had been used to tell many stories.

I began thinking about the simpler days of life, when typewriters were all we had. "Call waiting" and "Caller I.D."? What was that? If you weren't home, you didn't get the call. No computers, no iPods, no Facebook. I was out playing softball, building forts, or riding bikes with my best friend. I remember Mom always having the dinner on the table at 5:00 and we ate dinner together as a family every night. It was a time I looked forward to so much. Family, friends, fun. It was the simple things that made life so good.

I also remember prayer time each night with my family. I was tucked in every night by my parents and it was my time to share about the day. It was our time to end the day in prayer and pray for the next day ahead. Simple times shaped my entire life. It made Jesus so real to me. My focus was on Him....there just weren't all the distractions.

So as I sit here, yes, typing on my laptop while my iTunes are playing my favorite praise tunes... I am thankful, yet challenged. I am thankful for technology and the good things it has brought in life, yet challenged to focus on the simple things, the things that shaped my life in the first place. I am challenged to not spend as much time distracted by the technology, but more time quiet... quiet with Him. I am challenged to make life a bit simpler.

Have you ever found your life so busy that you are no longer enjoying the moment, but looking ahead at how you will manage the next task or event in life? Kind of takes the "simple" out of the equation doesn't it?

Just like that typewriter, I have many stories, and I hope many left to be written in my life. I want to savor the moments of them all. I want Jesus in all of them. I don't want to get so distracted that His presence is the last thing on my list. I want to focus on the things that matter. After all, when it is all said and done, it won't be the T.V. show that made a difference, it won't be a Facebook status, or a cool song from my iPod. It will be the time I took to spend with those I love... keeping it simple... keeping it joyful... .keeping it focused on the one who gave me this time in the first place. After all has been said... The greatest things in life aren't things. I couldn't agree more. I pray we all enjoy the simple things today, there are so many of them. You will be amazed at the hidden miracles God has waiting... in those very precious yet simple things in life.

Friday, February 17, 2012

Your Standing Ovation Awaits!

I sat there looking at that same tile floor, smelling that same sterile smell, and hearing the crinkle of the paper on the table as I swayed my feet back and forth. Ugh. It was another doctor visit and another anxious feeling for yet another test and another report. I thought to myself that a pity party would be in order about now. In fact I had so many emotions running around my head I found myself saying out loud "Jesus, help!"; "Hello? Anybody out there?"; "Lord? What is my purpose here?"; "What are you doing?" I had to almost chuckle to myself because I was firing one question after another as if He didn't already have the answer.

But then as I sat there in the quiet, I instantly knew... He was there with me. His presence all around. In fact I know He was holding me while I was sitting there on that table feeling sorry for myself. That sweet presence turned my many questions into breaths of praise. As I turned my mind toward Him, and got my mind off of myself and my fears I realized... He knows me. I mean He really knows me! Sounds simple, but really something changed in that moment. I began to rest in knowing... He had a purpose for me... even through all of this. I had purpose. How many times do we lose our purpose, and let go of our dreams because of fear, or a trial that comes our way that shakes us to the core?

When I was in my mother's womb, God was there. Though I may not have known Him, He knew me. He had a plan for me even then. Life is not so much a question of finding ourselves, but finding God. Really finding God... It is a question of discovering what God has already designed. When we find His purpose, we then understand how our uniqueness and gifts fit into what God is accomplishing. It's like a dramatic play that unfolds. This all was a part of that play. Even this visit to yet another doctor... all part of the play. In this play, the light is on us. Here's our cue! Most people miss their cues and they never realize they were in the middle of a divine appointment. God was there all the time...

It was then that God reminded me of everything I had been through... witnessed great miracles. I saw His hand in every situation. His grace carried me through each trial. He placed miracles at every turn... it was my job to look, expect, and trust. He had never let me down... why was I questioning?

God is a big thinker. My thoughts, even my big ones, are so small compared to God's thoughts. My dreams, even my biggest ones... pale in comparison to what God's dreams are for me. God-sized dreams are not man-made, they are God designed. God has shown me that if I find myself coming up with a plan, the dream is too small... When God chooses to confront a situation, He is a big thinker. When He looks at me, He already knows my background. He is not asking for my resume, He is asking me to be a servant He can trust. I needed to trust that His dreams and plans for me were beyond what I could even comprehend. Could I trust completely even in the tough times? Even when it looked like an impossible situation was in my path?

Was I able to trust? Was I committed? If I could be committed enough to do whatever it took, that is all God wanted. You can't give what you don't have. You can only give God your loaves and fishes. But most people hide their loaves because they don't really trust God. In order to fulfill God sized dreams, you need to be able to trust.

Someone asked me recently what this past year had taught me most. I can most definitely say it was all about trust. I daily remind myself that I want God's dream for my life. It may come in a different package that I think it will, but it is His dream and it is a wonderful dream. He is fully able to finish the dream. The question is will I finish with Him? Yes! I will finish with Him.

There are days I literally ask God to trust through me... because in my own strength I fail. He always brings me through stronger than ever.

Are you going through an impossible looking situation? Are you at that place where you feel like someone punched you in the gut and you just can't breathe for fear of what is ahead? Have you lost someone dear? Are you standing for the salvation for a loved one who is lost? Is your marriage or relationship hurting? Do you feel abandoned and alone? Are you dealing with secrets or addictions that torment your daily walk and some days paralyze you? Is the diagnosis you have been given by the doctor causing you to fight with the feelings to give up? God has not given up on you! He has a big dream for you and purpose. You have purpose! If you feel like you are on the end of the rope hanging on... Hang on! Your extreme is His opportunity. Remember... God is a big thinker! And His thoughts are on you! Even in the most dire situations... He is there. It is my prayer that in your journey to trust and dream that He gives you the supernatural strength to hang on.

By the time the doctor came in to give me the report... I knew no matter what, I was ok. I was smack dab in the middle of His dream for me, and that made it all worth it. It was good. It was worth trusting in. Trusting sometimes comes minute by minute, but it is worth it all. Your miracle will come. His presence will fill you, and the peace that passes all understanding will walk you through. And you will see... the spotlight that was on you in your play all along was Jesus. And this play, my friend, is worth a standing ovation! I hear the cheers already.

Thursday, March 29, 2012

It's rainy days like today that my memory takes me right back to precious time with my Grandma. She had a big bowl of buttons... each one had a story. She would help me string the buttons and make a necklace, telling me the story of each button and where it came from as we put each one on the string. How did she remember it all? Well I am glad she did because it's a beautiful memory I will never forget. I miss her. You never know when you are making life long memories for someone. Have a great rainy memory-making day!

Think I'll string some buttons :)

Friday, March 30, 2012

My Mom, My hero. I walk this journey with her, and what we have seen and learned together... I am forever thankful for. God shows up profoundly on those days when things change in an instant... and He proves that no matter what... He is a God of healing, hope, and ever sustaining peace. Just nothing like it.

Thursday, April 26, 2012

My party hat has been put to great use today. On my way out of the surgeon's office today I got in the elevator and a precious little girl with a beautiful smile and a pretty little hat tugged at my pants and asked if she could wear it. As she took off her pretty little hat, I saw she had lost much of her hair. She smiled so big as she put my party hat on. Needless to say, it is her party hat now. She was on her way to chemo, and she wanted to wear it to her appointment. I bent down and hugged her and she gave me one of the biggest bear hugs ever. I looked up at her Mom and she mouthed the words "Thank you". We both had tears running down our faces. Once again I am reminded of the things that really matter in life. God is in every moment if we let him be there. I don't want to miss one second of what He wants for me. Tomorrow I will once again have my party hat on as I sit with my own Mom as she starts her chemo appointments again. But regardless... with Jesus, everyday is a party. My heart is full. Party on!

Sunday, May 6, 2012

My heart is so full from such an amazing weekend I just wanted to go jump around in the yard and yell "Thank you Jesus". So I did.

Sunday, May 20, 2012

Love Wins

He was gruff, serious, and never talked. The neighbors always commented to me that they were scared of him. I knew there was a story here, and I prayed for him everyday as I ran by his house on my morning runs. I would see this man out mowing his lawn, never looking up, seeming very focused on the job at hand. He seemed sad.

One day as Holly and I ran by his house he was walking to his mailbox, and I stopped to say hello. I saw one of the neighbors watching as if they were horrified something bad would happen. His name was Bob. Bob immediately took up with Holly, who was my running buddy. Holly loved Bob! It was like she knew his story way before I did. Dogs are a great judge of character!

Turns out Bob was retired. He was then 65 years old and had served in the military almost all of his life. He seemed lonely, and made the comment "I think people are scared of me, and I don't have the energy to let them know I won't bite." Holly was a God-send on this visit. As he petted her, he began talking about stories in his life. And man did he have stories! War stories, childhood stories... my mouth was open in awe. People just didn't know Bob! He was one of the most caring, interesting people I had met in a long time! He had saved lives, and fought for our country in incredible ways! In fact, as we talked one day some fighter jets flew over us. He saluted with tears running down his face and said "That is music to my ears." He flew one... He saved lives and he had his life saved. Thank you God for our military. Do we thank them enough? I feel like we should express our appreciation to them daily! I thanked Bob. He said it had been a very long time since anyone recognized his service in the military. Wow.

His stories always led back to how much he loved dogs. I suggested he get one! Why not adopt a dog? He looked at me with surprise. I knew he was interested when I saw that sparkle in his eye. I told him about some places to adopt some great dogs, and a big smile crept on his serious, focused face. I do believe Bob had a very soft heart... and that softness was beginning to show!

I didn't see Bob for a few weeks, but as I ran by one day I saw him walking to his mailbox again. Following him was a big beautiful tan lab. He had adopted a dog and named him Max. Max had been trained quite well. His owner died suddenly and Bob came to the rescue... just in time! Bob's whole countenance had changed. Max sat by his side, and it was a match made in heaven. He said to me "I think Max was the one that did the rescuing. He rescued me, not the other way around."

Over the years Max and Bob became the neighborhood favorites. Bob trained Max to get the papers off the curb and take them to the door. Several times Holly joined Max. Max was one of the most obedient dogs I have ever seen. He always sported a bright collar or bandana, and Bob shined when he was with Max. It was such a blessing to see a hard shell come off of Bob, and see him set free. Bob often talked to me about God. I know these conversations were sent from the Lord. It was amazing. Bob got involved in a wonderful local church where he met his current girlfriend. Whoever says you can't have a girlfriend at 70 is wrong. They are so cute together!

I saw Bob this week... he flagged me down as I was running down the street. He had tears in his eyes, and my heart began to race. What happened? He began telling me about Max. Max had suddenly died. I was in shock. It was so fast that he literally fell into Bob's arms, gave one last tail wag and was gone. He had suffered a heart attack. At this point we were both crying. As the tears dried, Bob thanked me. He said the day I came to talk to him and suggested he adopt a dog, was the day his life changed. He was now engaged to his girlfriend, involved in a wonderful church, was involved in the community, and happier than he had ever been. He said Max was his angel here on earth. I could not agree more.

I have reflected on Bob and Max so much this week. I learned many things from this encounter. I learned that under the hardest of shells, there are people longing to be set free, loved and appreciated. Love wins. All the time, love wins. God uses that love to set people free. He even uses the love of a dog! I often think of what would have happened had I listened to the neighbors to "stay away from the scary man!" Bob was not scary. In fact he is a hero. A hero I am so thankful for. How many unsung heroes are out there wishing someone would listen to their stories? How many are hungry for just a simple "Hello"? Several years ago I set out to get to know my neighbors. I asked the Lord to help me. He did. He opens doors in ways I cannot. I thought this journey to get to know my neighbors would be a difficult and scary one. It has been one of the most fulfilling journeys of my life.

It is my prayer that we can all take a minute to listen, love, and be a friend to someone hurting. If you don't know how to start... just ask God. He will show you. He will open the doors. You will see it is a life changing journey, and yours is the life that will be changed the most! When I started thanking God for Bob's story... I instantly heard Him say to my heart... "You prayed for him every time you passed his house. I heard every one of those prayers." Why was I surprised? God knew just how to reach Bob's heart... and it started with a simple prayer and the love of a dog named Max.

Tuesday, June 5, 2012

"Freaky Fred"

His name was Frederick. I know this because I heard the neighbors call him one day. I call him "Freaky Fred". He was a spastic rat terrier who I truly believe plotted ways to make my daily runs as difficult as he could. I have to say this dog drove me nuts. He would pop out from nowhere barking and nipping at my ankles sometimes causing me to fall flat on my face. I have had many "Freaky Fred" falls. Fred loved to torment my dogs as we would run. One time he popped out from a bush and jumped on Holly's back. It was not a fun ride for Holly. Holly would look at me about a block before we would pass his house as if to say, "Oh please, don't make me run past Freaky Fred today!" We tried to change our running route, but Freaky Fred always found us. I was always so annoyed at the fact that the owners of this dog didn't watch him more closely.

A few weeks ago, I was determined to avoid our Freaky Fred encounter. I was alone on this run, and took a new route that I knew Freaky Fred would never figure out. As I was happily running along I was flagged down by a car. Inside the car was a little elderly man. As I got closer I could see he was crying. He said to me as he wiped the tears, "Miss, I know you run in our neighborhood a lot. We have lost our dog. We have looked for a day now and cannot find him." As we talked about descriptions I realized the dog he was describing was Freaky Fred! Holy cow! I have to say my first thought was "No more Freaky Fred Falls! Hooray!" But then my heart sank as I saw this sweet man wiping tears. I told him, I would indeed look for his dog. I was completely off my regular route and felt Fred would not be anywhere close. I began to pray for Fred... reluctantly, but I prayed. Then my heart had a turn of compassion for Fred and I wanted to find him! (That had to be God!) I was about 3 miles from where I spoke to Fred's owner, and as I was praying looked over and saw movement from behind a bush. I know God was in this passing glance. I never look at moving bushes when I run! I walked over and looked more closely and there was Fred! The little guy was shakin' in his boots and was frozen with fear. His spots were muddy, and he was scared. He was not jumping up like popcorn anymore, and he looked so pathetic. I looked at him and said, "OK Fred, it's you and me kid. We haven't been the best of friends, in fact I have quite detested you, but I think we need to change that." Fred would never let me near him in the past. He was always in attack mode so, I didn't know how this was going to end. I held out my hand and just sat there. Fred slowly peeked his dirty face out from the bushes, and proceeded to do the popcorn jump bypassing my hand and landing smack dab in my lap, licking my face as if to say "I surrender! I am sorry! You are my friend!" It was at that moment Fred became my buddy. We had about 3 miles back on route to get him home. I held Fred all the way. It was quite the bonding 3 miles I must say. It was then I realized, Fred had a story. I just didn't know what it was, but I was determined to find out.

As I walked up the hill, I saw the little elderly man standing in his driveway. I will never forget the moment that he saw me walking with Fred. He put his hands on his sweet face and in a quivering voice called out to me, "Is that Fred? Do you have our boy?" I waved to him and said "Yes! I found him!" I was determined not to cry at this point, but felt the tingle in my nostril, and that was it. The ugly cry began. I think back on that moment now and know it must have been quite a sight. A crying sweaty girl holding a muddy little rat terrier sobbing as I walked up the hill. Fred saw his owner and leaped out of my arms and the reunion began. (And my ugly cry became even uglier.) Many tears, and many barks were had that day. As I began to talk to the owner of Fred, I smiled as I listened to Fred's story. This elderly man was taking care of his wife who had Alzheimer's. They rescued Fred over a year ago. He had been abandoned, and when he was found had cigarette burns on his body, cuts, and had a bleeding neck from rope burns. They were Fred's saviors. They wanted to train Fred, but just had too many issues with their health that came up suddenly after they rescued him. They loved Fred in spite of his quirks... and there were many. When Fred was lost, his wife was distraught. She loved that little crazy dog. What would they do without Fred? As I walked into their backyard, I realized the small hole where Fred would make his daily escapes. The little man had no idea Fred was roaming wildly while he was inside taking care of his wife. We sealed up the hole and I looked at Fred. He was looking at me. He was really growing on me this Fred (who was named after the man's brother).

I spent several hours with this couple that day. I knew Fred's story now, and so much more. As I ran home after a wonderful time with this couple, I thanked God for Fred. God taught me so much through this little fella. Fred was "Freaky" for a reason. His hard exterior was a cover up of deep hurt and pain. His fear brought out something in him that was a type of protection for him. It was as if he was saying, "I have been hurt, and by golly you won't hurt me, in fact I'll get you first!"

How many Freaky Fred's have we had in our lives? How many times in life have we judged others too quickly not knowing their story? How many times have we been hurt or mistreated by others and left it as "Well, they are just mean people!" How many names have we called others who are different? Do we have people that rub us like sandpaper in life? It may even be family members. I wish I could say I never did this. I am guilty. I have been around very hateful people who have hurt me deeply and I just completely left the situation annoyed, and disgruntled, and just plain mad. What I failed to realize is that maybe all they needed was a kind word, love, compassion, time to hear their story. I could not hold a grudge because I did not know their story! Just like Fred, shaking in the bush, they are in the same position crying out for attention, yet covering up with a completely different behavior. Sometimes that behavior being what we may interpret as just plain mean and cruel. They have a story!

As I ran home I just asked God to forgive me for the many times I had labeled people who had hurt me as "Freaky Fred's". They were not freaky at all, they were fabulous! I just needed to love and look! I asked God to open my eyes and let me see what He was seeing in these people.

On my runs now, Fabulous Fred is always watching eagerly at the little window in the gate. His tail wags with glee when he sees me! I always go over and pet him and have a chat with him. In fact I decided that 1 or 2 days a week I would leave my dogs at home and go walk with Fred. I have had a chance to do some training with him, and he is quite the smart one! We are the best of buds now, and his owners and I are friends too! If you would have told me a few months ago, Fred and I would be friends, I would have never believed it.

God has a wonderful way of helping us turn Freaky into Fabulous! I challenge you to think of those in your life who totally annoy you, or who have hurt you. Pray for them, ask God for opportunities to change Freaky into Fabulous! You will be amazed how He reveals things and opens door for change... and usually the change begins in your own heart. It's pretty neat. I love these life changing journey's with God. I am always amazed how He teaches me lessons on these journey's in my life. And sometimes those lessons even come wrapped in the form of a little dog named Frederick. Bark on my friends, bark on!!!

Wednesday, June 20, 2012

There is just nothing more wonderful than the precious peace from the Lord in the middle of unexpected hurdles in life. Makes jumping over those babies a journey that in the end makes us better and stronger. I think that's neat.

Thursday, June 21, 2012

Standing in line getting an iced tea on the way to a day with Mom at her chemo appointment, behind me was a Mom talking to her daughter about how mad she was that the coffee here was so bad. She was also furious because she broke her nail. (And I truly mean furious.) As I listened to curse words bursting forth and the look on her daughter's face, my heart sank. The lady looked at me and said, "Do you know how I feel?" Surprised she even commented to me, I stood there silent for a moment. Before I realized what I was doing I put my arm around the woman and told her I was on my way to a chemo appointment for my Mom. She was taken back a little I could tell. I also told her that maybe a few years ago I may have complained about things, but through the journey I am on now with my sweet Mom, those things don't matter anymore. A bad cup of coffee? I'll take it. A broken nail... super glue. It's the seconds with my Mom that matter. When faced with the fragility of life and how fast things can change in an instant... life becomes precious. Jesus becomes more dear than ever... perspectives change... and what becomes a reality is that the things that really matter in life are not things at all.

Her name was Bridgette. I will never forget the look on her face as I talked to her about my sweet Mamma. She had a little tear in her eye, gave me a hug, took her coffee, apologized to me and her daughter for the outburst, and said... "Maybe this coffee isn't so bad after all... let's go get some superglue." She winked at me and said thank you. All I could do was smile and say "Thank you Jesus." As I sit beside my sweet Mamma today as she receives her chemo... I am just thankful for today. We are celebrating together, laughing together, and thanking God together... I sure do love her.

Sunday, July 1, 2012

Thank you, Lord, for life. And for silly laughter on days when it is much needed!

Wednesday, July 4, 2012

Friday, July 6, 2012

An early morning run with no iPod. Some mornings I just savor those runs in the quiet as I pray and listen. Today I am thankful for rest. The rest in the Lord that is ever sustaining. The rest that in any situation, no matter how big or small, how insurmountable, or difficult... it is overshadowed by victory in light of His presence... His rest. God has taught me more than ever this year that in His rest, all negativity is brought to a standstill. What a wonderful place to be! Have a restful day my dear friends!

Wednesday, July 11, 2012

Don't Look Back!

 He was a young man, and I had never seen him running in my neighborhood before. But on this particular day he was running the same route I was. I said "hello" to him as he passed, and he responded back with a very focused "hello". As he made it several blocks ahead of me I noticed that he kept looking back at something. I thought there might be a dog loose or something he may have seen that I did not. As I watched him running, admiring how fast he was going, all of the sudden as he was looking back, he lost his footing. He went crashing to the ground, hard. I gasped and took off running quickly to see if he was ok. As he got up, quite embarrassed, he just said to me, "That will teach me to look back!" And off he went, brushing himself off. I never saw this runner again, but I remember this day vividly. Why? I don't know. But it came back to my mind the other day as I was having my prayer time.

Have you ever felt like you are stuck in one place, unable to move forward? Have you cried out to God for an answer feeling like He is not hearing your cry? I think we have all felt this way at some time in our lives. I sure have. But what I realized more than ever, just like that runner who fell as he was looking back, is that I will be in the same position if I focus on what is behind me. I will miss what God has ahead for me if I am constantly reliving my past mistakes and focusing on things that happened years ago. Have you ever found yourself reliving past mistakes and past hurts like it was only yesterday? As I read my devotion this morning I came across this thought, and it reminded me of that runner, and the times I too focused on what was behind me rather than what was in front of me.

"If we choose to remain in a perpetual state of reliving our bad encounters, trials, mishaps, mistakes and tragic events we have experienced we become handicapped by the very thing we are trying to escape. It distorts our thinking and paralyzes us from breaking free of faulty mindsets and belief systems. It then becomes the primary source of the current state of problem or setback that we are encountering; further facilitating a continued fracture point in one's life."

How true it is! You see, where we put our thoughts, our energy, will have great impact on our forward movement and how we walk out our lives. One of my favorite verses is Proverbs 23:7 "As a man thinketh, so is he". It always reminds me to search my heart and find out where my focus really is during those difficult times when I feel overwhelmed. Am I focused on moving forward, or am I stuck? Am I focused on the Lord? Or am I focused on figuring it out myself? Am I focused on God's promises for my life? Or am I focused on lies and wrong information? What you focus on, you give life to. Where your energy is invested, multiplication occurs. What you behold, you become…

It is easy during the trials in life to forget who we are. We forget how deeply God loves us and is there for us. He is passionate about us! I love the passage 1 Peter 2:9-10. I have it where I read it often to remind myself of who I am! It declares God's heart over His people. It also provides direction in how to walk out that which He proclaims.

You are Chosen – Walk with the full understanding that you are cherished and loved.
You are a Royal Priesthood – Walk with an absolute knowledge that you are the sons and daughters of the King.
You are a Holy Nation – Walk embracing the gift of complete and full redemption that is yours in Christ.
You are God's Special Possession – Walk in confidence knowing that God is for you, that He has made you His own. That you are fully clothed in His mercy and grace and are positioned under the protective arm of the Father.

An important treasure to keep within your heart is this… it is not about what you don't have or don't like. Guard your heart always. Remember who you are. Remember "whose" you are!

One of my favorite songs of all time, and I will show my age on this one, was a song by Wayne Watson called, "Because of Whose I Am." I remember when the words to that song really sank in many years ago and I realized God had a plan for my life and it was good. I was His child and He really cared about me! As I look back on that day years ago, I see how He meshed all the events in my life, good and bad, to bring me to the place I am today. Even in spite of my mistakes, He worked miracles! He saw the painting as a masterpiece when all I saw were a bunch of colors running everywhere. He's the master painter after all, I just needed to give Him the brushes.

Let go of the past. It doesn't hold your present. In fact it will rob you of your present. Don't miss the miracles of today because your head is turned back. He's painting a masterpiece and when you get a glimpse of it... you will be blown away! Yes, you my friend are the son and daughter of a master creator! That just makes me want to shout a big yeehaw! Anyone want to join me? Let's remember "whose" we are today! Journey on my friends... journey on! Yeeehaw!

Thursday, July 12, 2012

I am amazed how often I am asked "Why do you love dogs so much?" God has opened more doors in my life... through dogs. Funny huh? In a nursing home visit with Holly, there was a precious 102 year old man. He was blind and he never came out of his room. He heard the dogs were there and even the nurses were excited that he wanted to come out and see them. Holly walked over and placed her head in the sweet man's lap. She looked up at him with a look that brought tears to my eyes. She knew... she just knew.

He began to pet her ears, and her face, and I saw a tear running down his cheek. Then he uttered some faint words... "I used to have a dog, this makes me feel like I am home. Oh those were good days." I could see by his face he was remembering some very sweet moments. He kissed her face and said "Thank you." Kleenex, please!

Dogs have a way of taking us home... to wonderful places in our lives... that we never forget. That day, Holly was an angel, if only for just a few minutes, to bring some happiness to a precious 102 year old man. Thank you God, for dogs, and for the doors you have opened because of them being in my life. Some of my best memories, biggest miracles, best friends, and best laughs have come because of them.

Pretty neat-o.

Thursday, July 19, 2012

My precious Mom. She's my inspiration. These chemo days are long for her, but our time together is sweet and I treasure every moment. Sometimes we laugh so hard we think they will kick us out of the chemo room. But usually we all end up laughing together. Some of the most amazing people I have met are hooked up to chemo, smiling and laughing and just thankful for each day. Oh the things I have learned on this journey with my Mamma. God is ever faithful and always...always with us. He truly never leaves us or forsakes us. I serve a miracle working God, and I am so thankful.

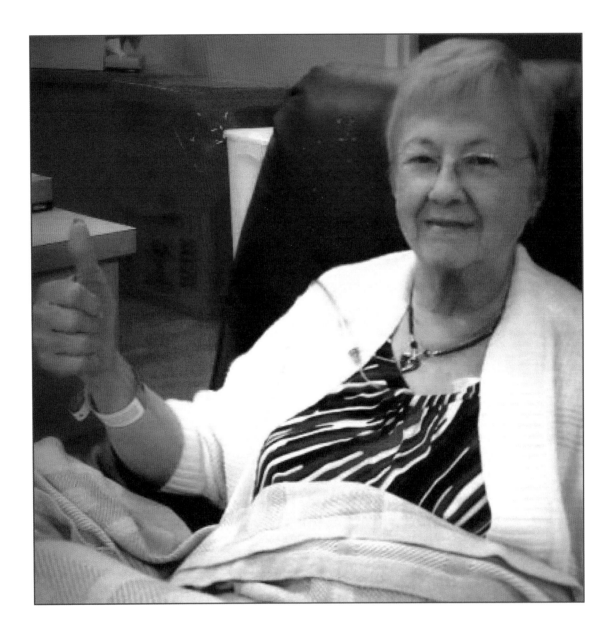

Sunday, July 22, 2012

Love Wins!

A few years ago, I asked the Lord to open doors for me in the area of getting to know my neighbors better. We have lived in the same home for 10 years, yet hardly knew anyone in our neighborhood. Isn't it funny how that happens? It was through that prayer that I began to meet and hear magnificent stories of those who lived around me. Beautiful friendships were born. Then it went further. I began to meet amazing people wherever I went. I heard stories that brought tears to my eyes, stories that made my heart leap with joy, stories that helped me pray more diligently for others, stories that made me thankful. I learned that behind every person is an amazing story. I learned that the people often judged the most by others, for a variety of reasons, truly have the most wonderful stories of all. Nobody really stopped to listen to them. They were too busy judging them, laughing at them, and passing them by. What beauty I have found, what amazing friendships have been made! What lessons I have learned! What miracles I have seen! What doors the Lord has opened!

When I thanked the Lord for answering my prayer by opening doors, I heard Him say to my heart, "Lisa, that open door was you looking....they were there all the time, you just didn't see them." Wow. How many things has God had in my path all along that I have missed because I was so focused on my day, my things, my life. It's amazing what happens when we just look for opportunities to be a blessing to others. What blessings await when we choose to love and not judge. Miracles are waiting at every turn.

Yesterday my miracle was a precious man in the grocery story, who had a beautiful story. Others were laughing at his overalls as he sat alone by the window. I adored those overalls (he called them his bib). They were chicken overalls, and yes... they had quite a story. He had such a wonderful sense of humor and was so joyful! He blessed my heart with the story of his overalls. I told him about my chicken suit and he loved it! We had the best conversation. He thanked me for talking to him and said he hadn't laughed that hard since he could remember. As I left that day I was so thankful for yet another amazing friend and another incredible story. And I was thankful I didn't miss the opportunity to hear it. It truly is life changing.

I want to challenge you to try it! Just spend a day looking for opportunities to be a blessing. Spend the day listening. I promise you, miracles will pop out from every corner. And what is neat about the journey is the biggest miracles begin within our hearts when we choose to love. Healing happens! Transformation begins! Old negative mindsets dissolve! Anger begins to fade! Walls come down! It's just so neat! Love wins every single time... it just does! Have fun on the journey! See you there! Love on my friends... Love on!

Wednesday, July 25, 2012

I taught Gracie to dance with me... now it's all she wants to do. She's got it right. No matter what comes in life, God can always give you the joy to dance. His joy truly is strength. Happy Dancing today my friends! May you find joy, even in places you never thought you'd find it. Dance on!

Thursday, August 2, 2012

Love those early morning calls with my sweet Mamma. I never take them for granted, and I treasure every single second. She's taught me through her journey... savor the seconds. Don't waste time. There's joy and miracles in it all, even in the hard journeys... just look for it. God is bigger... He's just bigger... no matter what. Love wins. Laugh. If you are feeling down, go out and bless someone; those feelings will turn around through giving. Be thankful... there is always something to be thankful for. The things in life that truly matter are not things. She fights this cancer journey with a faith in God that has forever touched me and those around her. But that's who she is. I love her.

Friday, August 3, 2012

We will always find what we are made of in life when we encounter the storm.

Tuesday, August 14, 2012

Why We Need "Underwear" Friends!

I just read a devotional this morning that has now become my favorite. It's about underwear friends!
(I know, right?!) These special friendships are there when the wedgies of life tear us apart at the seams.
It made me think about all the amazing people God has placed in my life... my friends.

I have friends that lift me up, support me, even pinch me back to reality when I go out in left field. They have stood with me, laughed with me, been patient with me, prayed with me, cried with me, and even drove me around while wearing a chicken suit! I have learned so much from my friends. They are treasures who enrich my life. The best kinds of friends in life are those who love us despite our wrinkles and warts. They have a knack for drawing the best out of us and challenging us to grow into all we were meant to be in our journey of life and faith.

Psalms 18:39 is one of my favorite verses: "You have equipped me with strength for the battle..."

I thank God for my underwear friends; they lift, support, squeeze, and even pinch me if necessary. They are God's resources that gird up my proverbial loins for the battle. I can throw away my girdle, because they are the best option to gird me up... God's option. A friend is one of the best things you can have and one of the best things you can be. I want to be the best friend I can be. I want to give back what I have so generously been given.

We are on a mission!

I am forever grateful for my underwear friends! They have made life's wedgies a journey I have grown through and seen miracles through. May we all be underwear friends! Stretch on my friends... stretch on!

Friday, August 17, 2012

It's a Great Day! I Say We Jump!!!

Sunday, August 19, 2012

Happy Birthday to My Sweet Mamma

Another year to celebrate my hero. Mom, I love you so much.

Tonight we celebrated my sweet Mamma's birthday. It doesn't get sweeter. My heart is full.

Tuesday, August 21, 2012

What a Friend We Have ….

She sat there with a look on her face that was angelic. I remember it like it was yesterday. She would sit in her rocking chair and sew for hours. Those clothes she worked so hard on, would be sent to missions. She usually had a straight pin or two in her mouth, but it didn't stop her from singing. I could hear the shaky sweet voice of my precious Grandma sing "What a friend we have in Jesus, all our sins and griefs to bear. What a privilege to carry everything to God in prayer." It was her favorite hymn. There are days that sweet tune she sang rings in my spirit for hours.

This week as I sat here thinking about the journey I am on, I started to get a little overwhelmed. Never at one time have I ever had so many huge tasks at hand that needed so much faith, and endurance. I am a doer. I am a planner. I tend to over-think things in figuring out how things will work. This can work for me at times, and it can work against me at other times. Have you ever become so exhausted in the planning that you don't enjoy the trip? Well I found myself working on the solution to every situation, and there were many situations to be solved. It was exhausting.

Then as I sat there completely overwhelmed, there it was. It was that sweet shaking voice that sounded like an angel. It was like it was right there with me. I just remembered it all and began to sing it outloud. "What a friend we have in Jesus, all our sins and grief to bear. What a privilege to carry everything to God in prayer." The hymn my Grandma would sing for hours. It rang so strongly in my spirit, and a peace came with it.

I remember even as a young girl I would get overwhelmed, and my Grandma would remind me to stop looking at the problem, look to Jesus. She said it with such comfort. It was so simple, so sweet, so life-changing.

As I sung the song under my breath, I realized that all my methods to solve, all my plans, all my "trying to figure things out", won't work without His fingerprints on them. He reveals to me what doesn't work because, after all, He is the answer. In my worthy goals to do things right, and figure things out, in my home, school, church, ministry, relationships, in any place or situation, there is no saving grace, no answer, apart from Jesus. It is Jesus alone that makes the difference. His competence, His comprehensiveness, His assessment of what is needed, His interactions in hearts, and in days, His presence and performance are key to any "solutions."

I cannot over-think God's plan, I need to trust Him with it. As C.S. Lewis said "Relying on God has to start all over every day, as if nothing has yet been done." Some days that means relying on Him minute by minute.

Oh the amazing things I have learned on this journey. He shows up in ways I never dreamed. He teaches me and equips me in some of the hardest times of my life. I think that is so neat. It's not about me, and how I can fix things. It's about Him and how I can trust His plan, no matter what.

As I sing that song over and over in my captive consciousness: "What a friend we have in Jesus, all our sins and griefs to bear. What a privilege to carry everything to God in prayer." I am not singing anymore about my act of carrying anything, or figuring things out, or my acts at all. I am singing about Him. He's the game-changer, He's the difference maker.

Are you facing something that seems insurmountable? Let God put His fingerprints on it, let Him be the game changer for you. He is there just waiting. Not only will you see your breakthrough, you will watch your life be transformed through the journey with Him. You will love who you become! What a friend we have in Jesus! I will forever hear this hymn in my heart. Thank you Grandma, for so lovingly instilling in me what this really means. I know she is in heaven smiling and singing. And I kind of think heaven joins in with her when I sing those sweet words.

What a Friend we have in Jesus,
all our sins and griefs to bear!
What a privilege to carry
everything to God in prayer!
O what peace we often forfeit,
O what needless pain we bear,
All because we do not carry
everything to God in prayer.

Have we trials and temptations?
Is there trouble anywhere?
We should never be discouraged;
take it to the Lord in prayer.
Can we find a friend so faithful
who will all our sorrows share?
Jesus knows our every weakness;
take it to the Lord in prayer.

Are we weak and heavy laden,
cumbered with a load of care?
Precious Savior, still our refuge,
take it to the Lord in prayer.
Do your friends despise, forsake you?
Take it to the Lord in prayer!
In His arms He'll take and shield you;
you will find a solace there.

Blessed Savior, Thou hast promised
Thou wilt all our burdens bear
May we ever, Lord, be bringing all to
Thee in earnest prayer.
Soon in glory bright unclouded there
will be no need for prayer
Rapture, praise and endless worship will be our sweet portion there.

 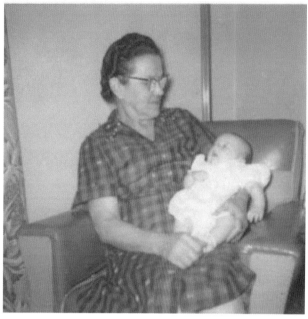

Friday, August 24, 2012

Joy in Dark Places… With a Party Hat.

It was not the news I was expecting. In fact as I sat listening to the test results for my sweet Mamma, hearing that her cancer was no longer responding to the chemo, it was as if someone had placed a plastic bag over my head and I was suffocating. The house was quiet. Everyone was gone for the day and I listened to the silence. Is there a word to describe what I felt? If there is I don't know what it was. As fast as all the questions filled my head was as fast as my lips just kept uttering the words "Jesus help."

All I could get out was a faint whisper... "Jesus help." It came from a place in my soul that had never cried out like that before. In an instant... the sweetest presence blew over me and I knew He was there. Where I ended... He began. Someone asked me the other day, "How does this Holy Spirit thing work for you?" They asked me if it really was possible to have joy in the dark places. Today, sitting in a dark place... He's there. It's as if the room lit up and I didn't have to ask the questions because I knew He had the answers and they all made sense. That, my friend, is the Holy Spirit. That is what gives me joy to jump, joy to face this journey with my sweet Mamma, joy to know there is a party to be had on this side of heaven... regardless of what my circumstances are.

As we drove to the Doctor today, knowing what we were facing... or better yet, not knowing what we were facing... we looked at each other and we laughed! I know right? We were cracking up! Belly laughs! We hugged each other in the car as we sat parked in the lot and we remembered the scripture the Lord gave us through this journey. Jeremiah 33:3 "Call on my name and I will answer. I will show you great and mighty things you know not of." We felt joy! We felt expectant, and we felt a party coming on. And you know me, I always have party hats in tow and by golly we wore them to this appointment. Whatever the news... God had a party in store.

The news was not that great. One more try at chemo, and then we take a look at things. Another plan to be tried. The doctor never knows what to expect when Mom and I come to see him. In fact he always opens up the door and peeks in first. And then he smiles. I say "Come join the party!" We love it when we make him laugh. It's kind of become our mission.

I am sitting here with my precious Mamma now. That red bag of chemo running into her veins... it's a love hate relationship. I have prayed as it enters her body the blood of Jesus heals her. I pray we will see those great and mighty things we know not of. No matter what, we have had the journey of our lives. We have been able to minister, love, pray for, and cheer those on who are in this battle with her.

A precious beautiful young lady sitting beside Mom is having a rough journey. The tears are flowing and she is heartbroken. All I could do was put my hand on her leg and pray. She asked me for a party hat. Do I have an extra one? Are you kidding? I have a bag full! As I watched her tears dry and the laughter began... I just thanked God for the journey He has us on. It's a journey of party hats! That even in the hardest journeys, we see the biggest miracles. The laughter we heard today, no money can buy. Moments like these are those that shape and define and stay in our hearts forever.

The lessons I have learned on this journey with my Mamma have changed me forever. Jesus has become more real and closer than ever. His Spirit and His presence have carried me when I felt uncarriable. I am thankful He has His party hat on too. I know when we get to heaven... it's going to be one huge party. Why not start now? Today... we are. Yes, even in the chemo unit. But that's just Jesus. That's just my precious Jesus. And that my friend is why I jump for joy....a lot! Party on!!!

Made in the USA
Lexington, KY
03 January 2013